Make Me an Offer I Can't Refuse

street-smart "gangster" rules for your working life

by Susan Riehle

think
upside
down™

Copyright © 2014 Susan Riehle All rights reserved.

No part of this publication may be reproduced, stored in a retrieval system, or transmitted in any form or by any means, electronic, mechanical, photocopying, recording, scanning, or otherwise, without the prior express written permission of the author.

Limit of Liability/Disclaimer of Warranty. The author makes no representations or warranties with respect to the accuracy or completeness of the contents of this book and specifically disclaims any implied warranties or claims.

 Think UpsideDown ™

www.thinkupsidedownbooks.com

Library of Congress Cataloging-in-Publication Data

Riehle, Susan
MAKE ME AN OFFER I CAN'T REFUSE, street-smart "gangster" rules for your working life / Susan Riehle—1st ed.

ISBN 978-0-9913592-0-2 (paperback)

1. Vocational guidance. 2. Quality of work life. 3. Success in business. 4. Career development. 5. Negotiation in Business

Contents

FOREWORD i

INTRODUCTION —WHY GANGSTERS? vii

CHAPTER 1—YOUR MONEY OR YOUR LIFE
CAREER STRATEGY 1

CHAPTER 2—A MADE MAN
INTERVIEWING 15

CHAPTER 3—AN OFFER I CAN'T REFUSE
NEGOTIATING SALARY 37

CHAPTER 4—GOODFELLAS
THE VALUE-ADDED EMPLOYEE 57

CHAPTER 5—YOU TALKING TO ME?
CONFLICT RESOLUTION 73

CHAPTER 6—FORGETTABOUTIT
TOUGH SITUATIONS 85

CHAPTER 7—MAKE MY DAY
THE ART OF BEING ACCIDENTALLY LUCKY 103

EPILOGUE 115

BOOK EXCERPT
THE ENLIGHTENED ENTREPRENEUR 119

WISE GUYS TIPS
QUICK REFERENCE GUIDE 145

Special Thanks to

Aliyah Marr,
Karen Parker, and
Michelle Riehle,
who spent lots of
hours checking my
work and who
believed in this book.

Foreword

With an intriguing "gangster" theme, Susan Riehle uncovers little known strategies for career-seekers that employ the use of self-evaluation, problem-solving, and careful planning. She takes a look at "the other side of the coin" and assists readers in understanding the interview from the employer's perspective.

Most importantly, she offers an interview plan and six-step process that are easy to follow and ensures that the interviewee is properly prepared for each and every interview. The author recounts stories from her personal career journey and those of others who she has coached through career transitions that readers can relate to and which further illustrate her methodology for career planning.

Throughout her work, tips are shared on everything from effective interview responses to salary negotiations, understanding personality types, and conflict resolution. This is more than just your ordinary career advice. This is unique LIFE advice that can only be learned through trial and error, careful observation, and really listening to the stories people tell about their career trials and tribulations.

With a little something for everyone, and a whole lot more for the individual who is truly ready to advance, change, restart, or breathe new life into their career, this ingenious book is not one that should be missed.

—Melissa Parker Dean, Harrison College, Columbus Campus

Make Me an Offer I Can't Refuse

Introduction: Why Gangsters?

Why Gangsters?

> *"If you hold back anything, I'll kill ya. If you bend the truth or if I think you're bending the truth, I'll kill ya.*
>
> *If you forget anything, I'll kill ya. In fact, you're gonna have to work very hard to stay alive, Nick.*
>
> *Now do you understand everything I've said? Because if you don't, I'll kill ya."*
>
> —Rory Breaker, "Lock, Stock & Two Smoking Barrels"

Why gangsters? Gangsters are the original countercultural force in life as well as in fiction. As Al Capone put it, "Capitalism is the legitimate racket of the ruling class." And looking at capitalism as a racket lets us see the inside gimmicks and tricks that allow us to 'win against the house' and against all odds.

Gangster quotes are simple, direct and—ironically—in many ways dead-on correct about legitimate business. Without pulling any punches, these original bad-asses of business point out the stupid quirks of getting and keeping a job.

Besides, Gangsters are fun! They certainly weren't fun in life, but they have a funny side in death and fiction. Job-hunting and job-keeping are serious business—just as serious as a mob boss—so you can use a little humor.

And, finally, I have to ask you to change yourself to be able to get that better job. Change is hard for people—I need backup and I call upon "Lucky," and Al and Dillinger and Butch. As Charlie "Lucky" Luciano says—

"We have a problem. Our problem is you…"

You have to change, in order to change your luck. So I'll endeavor to not hold anything back in giving you the best advice that you don't read in other books.

Chapter 1: Career Strategy

Your Money or Your Life

Jack Benny skit…

*A robber tells Jack Benny,
"Give me your money or your life."*

*The great comedian Jack Benny paused,
and the studio audience—knowing
just how cheap he was—laughs.*

*The robber demands again, "Look, bud!
I said your money or your life!"*

Benny replies, "I'm thinking it over!"

Do you feel as though your job makes you choose between making money and having a life? Don't settle! You can have both.

Strategic Career Planning! Does that term scare you? It doesn't need to. A job is a source of money. To most people the more money the better. However, it may be your goal to make money—while enjoying what you do. It's not "Your Money or Your Life." It's how to make money—while still enjoying your life.

And yet, it's been difficult to find work, and even harder to find satisfying work in the last few years. Many people now think this is the new normal.

How do you identify what skills an employer will pay you for? How do you find work you will enjoy? It begins with asking yourself some critical questions and then answering them honestly. Now, some reading this will say, "Realistically, not everyone can have a fun job, after all no one pays you for work they want to do!"

There is realism and there is fear. You may or may not find work that leaves you dancing in the street, but you can certainly find work that leaves you smiling at the end of the day.

"I never lie because I don't fear anyone. You only lie when you're afraid."—John Gotti

Not attempting to get the best work you can for a good wage, is a sign of fear of change. Ask yourself, what or who are you afraid of?

Looking for a way to enjoy your workday is no risk at all. If you answer a few simple questions honestly, you can fearlessly pursue both a good wage and a good working life. It's the beginning of *Strategic Career Planning*.

Chapter 1: Career Strategy

Let me tell you about "Hal." Hal is a friend that I've been talking with about his career path (we used to work together). He's been working for a number of years, professionally since the late 70s.

Lately he's had some job upheavals and has worked some contract jobs. His current contract was up and he was involved in a job search for the next contract job.

Ahh, the life of a contractor! He'd like to work 1-2 more contract jobs, and then go 'direct.' He's hoping that one of the contract jobs will be his dream job and go direct from that job. He doesn't know how to make that happen.

'Yes,' he networks; 'Yes,' he's on LinkedIn; 'Yes,' he's listed his contacts and called them (once) and 'Yes,' he talks to headhunters when he can't avoid it. His main technique of job hunting is firing off resumes to jobs listed on the job boards.

Hal is typical of a guy who finds it hard to be job hunting. For him the easiest course is the anonymous emailing of a resume. Hal is typical of someone whose strategy has gotten lost in his need for a job.

Would it surprise you to know that only a few of job placements happen from resumes emailed to jobs posted on job boards? If that's true, then logic tells you that Hal's odds of finding a job is slim if this is his main technique.

Where should Hal begin? Well the conventional wisdom is that Hal ought to examine his skills and values. Once he knows who he is and what he has to offer.

He then ought to do an analysis that shows him what to do next. Hal's an Engineer so this all sounds like Human Resources nonsense to him. He was resisting any attempt to get him to do this stuff.

So we took a very different approach. I asked him to tell me about a time when he was happy, or proud of something. He offered to type that up for me when he found his answer—he meant that in interviews he'd been asked a question like that and had prepared a behavioral interviewing type answer.

I stopped him, "No, I wasn't asking an interview question." When was he happy at work or at home? What in his whole life made him happy, or proud or satisfied?

> *"I'm no saint, but I swear to you that I'm no bum either." —Frank Cotroni*

His first answer was that there was a time at work that he was happy because he was able to bring together a whole lot of skills to handle a problem. He really felt he contributed. His second answer was: when his kids were still at home.

Chapter 1: Career Strategy

I laughed and said, "You are empty-nesting." He went on to talk about something else: he said that in general he felt happiest when he had a very different project to do when he got home—not work related.

And last of all he told me about a time when he used to work in different countries. He's been longing to travel again.

In that short conversation we found some important things that Hal could use as a basis of his strategic career direction: He's a generalist and is happiest as a generalist, where he can use many different skills he's learned in different places.

He needs a strong separation between work and home, so he needs to leave work at work after a 40-50 hour week.

This is fortunate for Hal because contractors are paid by the hour, supporting his desired schedule. And unlike most people he wouldn't mind a significant amount of travel.

And he wouldn't mind if his work somehow included kids, really. Neither he nor I see this fitting in, but we'll keep it in mind.

These stated preferences form the basis for Hal's conclusion that being contractor is fine for him for the moment. He also knows that he can search jobs that seek someone who may travel—which gives him an edge on competitors.

Tip 1—The key to strategic planning: "Know Thyself"

You could analyze yourself and you might determine your values, hopes and dreams through a lengthy analysis—or you could do what I did with Hal:

Ask yourself when you were most happy. Write down the honest answer (not the interview question answer you dreamed up). Then ask yourself: what about that time made you happy?

Tip 2—Another way to understand your values is to think about whom you admire

I could also have asked him about people he admired and maybe found similar answers. There are no wrong answers. But there are too specific conclusions.

Hal has lots of years of experience, but his career has wandered over several different fields. Perhaps this is true of you: You started in a direction and then got promoted or transferred into different areas. After a decade of so, you've ended up in a vastly different job than you started in. Maybe that's good, but maybe not.

Do you like what you do? Do you like how you spend your day? Are you proud of what you do? If not, maybe it's time to seek a different direction.

In our example, Hal now knows a few things to help him narrow his search. However, he has a new

Chapter 1: Career Strategy

problem: It's tough to balance what you want with what options you have. What if Hal can define the position he wants but can't find it?

So far we've talked generalities, but not real job qualifications. Traditional advice would be to now look at his Strengths, Weaknesses, Opportunities and Threats (Businesses do an analysis called a SWOT analysis based on this). But that is just not how real people think about strategizing a career.

When people try to look at complex situations like Hal's situation of wanting to find a job that makes him happy and still having to balance that with what jobs are out there available to him—people get stuck. It's easy to choose between a hamburger and a cheeseburger; it's hard to choose between a wide-open field of job choices.

Tip 3—It's easy to identify strengths and weaknesses by examining what you liked in past jobs

Hal needs a way to quickly figure out some balance between the opportunities that are available and what direction he is going. It's tough to choose between lots of things, but easy to choose between two things, so that's what we did. I'd pick two things from his resume that were related. Hal liked A better than B and C better than A. In Hal's case this boils down to a choice between working with one programming language or another or a choice might be between automotive and healthcare industries.

In your cases it could be between working on a large team or a small team and working with scheduling or accounting tasks.

As you ask yourself which task you prefer. Then ask yourself why? Is it because you feel you have more experience or more interest?

Is it a strength, or just better because it's not a weakness? Similarly, Hal could just as easily compare choices in job descriptions on a job board two at a time.

Tip 4—Ask 'Why?' A technique anyone can use

Another way to identify strengths and preferences in jobs is to employ an old management trick. Ask yourself what was your favorite job. Then ask "Why?" Whatever you answer, ask again, "Why?" Repeat.

By the time you get to the fifth "why," you will normally have answered something that reveals a strength or preference. This technique is easiest to employ with a friend.

The beauty to this approach is that as you learn about your choices, you are also preparing yourself to explain your choices. In Hal's case that could be used immediately as he answers job interview questions.

Chapter 1: Career Strategy

In your case, it can help you identify your strengths, and weaknesses. People naturally gravitate toward their strengths, liking jobs where they feel they can use their strengths. People naturally gravitate away from weaknesses and the jobs where they feel they will do badly.

Tip 5—Successful people build on strengths

Now here's something counter-intuitive: remediate what you must of your weaknesses, but move toward your strengths. School has it wrong. Schools focus on your weaknesses.

But consider that neurosurgeons don't become neurosurgeons because they are bad in science. Writers don't become writers because they are bad in English. Yes, you might need to remediate a bad weakness, but successful people build on strengths.

Repeat your strengths to yourself, write them down, repeat them to everyone you meet. Remember this is who you are. Before you can take the next step you need to think about what you know.

Using Hal as an example: Hal now knows what industry he prefers; the skills he wants to use; the term of employment; and a strategic advantage that he has over other workers. He's at a place to be able to articulate to an employer or 'headhunter' what he prefers.

Hal will certainly be asking headhunters what's available. He will also ask what jobs are tough to fill. He will ask about the challenges that agents are having in filling jobs. These will be his opportunities.

If you are not actively seeking a job, you are ready to find opportunities. You will be looking to see what you can do, which others cannot.

How can you redefine your job? What work can you ask for? What is your company not able to do easily? What dumb things are they doing? In short you look for what opportunities do you see that your strengths could address.

I find these opportunities in the oddest places. I'm good at matching up people to solutions. So for me a lunch with a friend is rarely wasted. Even a coffee with an acquaintance is rarely wasted.

Generally I find that I can make a connection between two people that I know if I ask an occasional question. One of my favorite questions is to ask people to tell me their greatest challenge at work. I find my personal satisfaction goes up each time I can solve someone's challenge.

We've talked about Strengths and Opportunities, What about Threats? A business talking about a SWOT analysis would use threats to identify things that might derail a business—supplier defaults, cash shortages, regulation changes.

Chapter 1: Career Strategy

For Hal the threats are also something he and I have discussed. He's past fifty and age-ism exists in technical fields. He also knows he could get stuck in shorter and shorter contract positions.

He also could find himself in a job that limits his exposure to new technology and so makes him out-of-date.

For you similar risks exist. If you aren't looking at your career strategy, you may never be forced to face the threats until you lose a job or get stuck in a dead-end job.

Examining your 'threats' allows you to look ahead and around corners. Every employee ought to have a career strategy that they review periodically for opportunities, career satisfaction and for 'threats.' If you aren't taking steps to address 'threats' you are missing a key part of a career strategy.

Typical actions to take include continuing education, awareness of career interests, maintaining contacts. Not so typical choices might be volunteering (expands your sources of information, showcases your skills to others), taking up a new hobby, mentoring somebody else.

So what's the plan?

Your life would be very sad if it only included a plan for a career. Your happiness at work is linked to your happiness at home. As Hal mentioned, some of what made him happy happened after he left work. If you don't integrate your work goals and home goals chances are that you will not feel satisfied. A person feels soulless when they only have work goals and no personal ones.

It's like dieting. How does one succeed at dieting? First you have a plan. Second you incorporate that plan into your daily life. Third, you make sure that it works with your lifestyle—so you can continue to work toward your goals.

Have a plan and consider in it what is important to you at home. Remember that your happiness and satisfaction counts. If you like what you do, you will do it better.

> *"All my life I wanted to be a bank robber. Carry a gun and wear a mask. Now that it's happened I guess I'm just about the best bank robber they ever had. And I sure am happy."*
> *—John Dillinger*

Chapter 2: Interviewing

A Made Man

"Capitalism is the legitimate racket of the ruling class." —Al Capone

Does interviewing for a job seem like a racket? Do you sometimes feel nervous or awkward in interviews? Do you ever come out of an interview with no clue whether you did well or not? Do you want to know how to always interview well? You can!

Q: How to ace an interview?
A: Think strategically

Thinking strategically is the single most important thing an interviewee can do. You could run two dozen people from a graduating college class through two dozen interviews with two dozen different interviewers for similar jobs. Chances are most of the interviewees would get a job offer.

A few would be offered several jobs. And one or two might not get offers. You can draw several conclusions from this. First, there are lots of opinions about who is best suited for any one job. Second, you can either do well in an interview or not. Third, not everybody gets a job in every interview.

> *"If you think your boss is stupid, remember: you wouldn't have a job if he was any smarter."* —John Gotti

Many folks are intimidated by interviews, because they assume that there is someone clearly better prepared than they are for the job. If that were true, in my example of two dozen people, interviewers and interviews one person would be offered two dozen jobs!

In a graduating class of engineers only the top student would get all the job offers! In a graduating class of journalists the worst student wouldn't have a chance of getting a job!

In the real world, that top student gets more offers, but not all offers. And in the real world even the worst student has a chance at a job—if he/she can interview well and is persistent.

And while you, as an interviewee, are intimidated, so is the interviewer. Surprised?

Research shows that the interviewer is nearly as nervous as the interviewee! While the research doesn't say why, I suspect that it's because very few interviewers feel confident about interviewing. He/she doesn't feel

Chapter 2: Interviewing

they know what to ask and what to look for in the answers. So relax.

Q: SO WHAT IS THE MAGIC WAY TO INTERVIEW?
A: THE KEY TO INTERVIEWING WELL IS TO PRESENT WHAT IS UNIQUE ABOUT YOU FOR THIS JOB

There really is only one question that you answer in an interview. No matter what you are asked, you answer a variation of this question. That question is: "Why should I hire you and not the next person I interview?"

If you can answer that question you will interview better. An interviewing better tilts the odds in your favor. It may never guarantee you a job, but it does improve your odds.

If the interviewer asks, "Tell me about a time when you handled a tough situation at work?" What they are really asking is, "How will you handle a tough situation in THIS job?"

So, give an example from your past, which is relevant to problems, which you might encounter in this job. The best answer will be something that emphasizes your unique strengths.

That's where the strategic thinking comes in: You can only answer that question well, if you know what you uniquely bring to the table.

Resist being a jack-of-all-trades—be a specialist, and just the right specialist

A common mistake is to be everything to everybody. Perhaps you've applied to every job that you could find. Perhaps your resume has a very vague purpose section. Ask yourself, do most employers want someone who *can* do the job well, or someone who *will* do the job well?

Most people read resumes literally. Most people interpret answers to interview questions literally. The closer your resume and interview responses get to the exact problems encountered in this job, the better your odds of getting the job.

It's easiest to think about this in a slightly cynical way. Most people interviewing for a job will offer the job to someone who is doing almost exactly the same job already.

So they will offer the job of an artistic director to someone who already in a job as an artistic director. Why? Because it's easy to be sure they will do the job well.

An emergency care nursing job is most obviously be offered to someone who has been an emergency care nurse! A senior corporate accounting job is most likely to be offered to someone who has been a senior corporate accountant. Are you already interviewing for the job that you have? Probably not. So what do you

Chapter 2: Interviewing

do? You pick the items in your resume that are similar to the job you are interviewing for and make these items more prominent. Move them to the top, or into main descriptions.

When interviewing, pick stories to talk about in response to questions that are most similar to the situations found in the job you are interviewing for. Show that you are not only a specialist, but you are just the right specialist.

But wait! What about Hal- the example given in the last chapter? Hal was a 'generalist.' Don't get caught up in these terms. Hal needs to be exactly the 'right kind' of generalist. He has to show he has the right skills for the job. For instance, it would be most powerful for Hal to show that he has two specific skills that are hard to find together.

> Think about the interviewer's problems and answer their questions while showing that YOU solve their problems

Interviewers have two types of problem that candidates solve. The first has to do with technical qualifications, the second deal with people problems. Ironically, job seekers prepare for the first, but experienced hiring managers look first at the second. It's easy to understand why the experienced managers worry about the people problems.

If you have ever hired someone who lied, drank, fought or didn't show up, you'd feel burned. And you would always check for these problems first.

For technical qualifications

You can do research to find out what they want. Ask someone who works there what software they use. Research the company on the web. Read the job postings; note the keywords.

For generic people concerns

Think like a hiring manager. I've supervised a drunk, a thief, someone who caused infighting; someone who didn't show up for work; someone who was too good to do certain work; someone who lied; someone who wouldn't learn new skills; someone who was incompetent; someone afraid to take chances. The hardest of those to deal with was the liar.

All of these speak to an employer's biggest problem: trust. The interviewee who inspires trust has a key strategic advantage.

I especially want people who can solve problems, work independently and grow. So if you can show me that a previous employer gave you increasing responsibility—that is golden.

Someone with increasing responsibility has the previous employer's trust. If your previous boss trusted you, then I will feel I can too. You have demonstrated that I can trust you.

You can show that you have your former employer's trust by spotlighting that in a resume. On your resume, in the job listing that is closest to the job you are trying for, be sure to have something that shows you have your boss' trust. Training others, responsibility for money, responsibility for a key project all show that trust.

In an interview, you show your prior boss's trust by the 'stories' you tell. A truthful, real-life example where you took on responsibility and handled work to the conclusion of a project is ideal.

Such an example shows not only skill, but initiative and ability to manage time and resources—it says to a boss, this person is easy to manage.

Who tells the interviewer how to interview?

There really isn't much training. An interviewer may be handed a sheet of standard questions, but rarely more than that. For those few that get training, it's predictable what they are told.

I've done an informal survey. About one third of interviewers only really check the employment dates for discrepancies. Another third try to guess whether the person interviewing will be a good fit on the team. The last third stumble along, and frequently seem to compare the person to themselves—sometimes even competing with them!

A few who get real professional training, are told that the interview goal is to establish team 'fit' and real experience level.

In other words the professionally trained interviewer will try to establish: Can you play nicely with others? Are you truthful? Are you reliable? How much experience do you really have?

These trained or prepared interviewers will typically ask behavioral interviewing questions: these are the open-ended response questions like, "Tell me about a conflict at work." They are looking for complete and consistent answers.

Help! How can I show 'trust' when my current boss is a micromanager?

Don't lie and don't call your current boss a micromanager in the interview. Simply state that one reason you are looking for a new position is to take on new challenges and responsibilities. Pick a different true example from your life that shows a supervisor or team trusted you.

Chapter 2: Interviewing

What do you do well?

Most people know what they do well. If you don't, then think about what you can prove you do well—show up for work? Take responsibility? A certain skill?

Credibility & trust—a winning combination

The candidate that can show skills is a strong candidate. But how is a boss to know whether the 'stories' are real? This gets us to credibility.

Let's talk about an easy beginner error: Jen's interview is going great. The interviewer asks a question. Jen answers that question and illustrates her answer with a great story about a prior job with some specifics built in. The interviewer looks down at the resume and can't find the job on the resume. Does that interviewer believe her story?

Most people realize that Jen did two things right and one wrong. She had a story to back up the answer. That story corroborates Jen's answer by showing she walks the walk, not just talks about doing something.

She also had specifics in her story so that it is heard like a memory. The interviewer could see that experience through Jen's eyes. The more the interviewer sees Jen in the job in their mind's eye, the more the interviewer can see Jen in the new job. But then Jen made the error too. She didn't tie the 'story' to a position that can be verified on her resume. Your goal is to build trust and credibility. Jen built that trust in her spoken answer and undermined it in her resume.

It's simple
- ✧ Simple answers are best—the ones that illustrate your strengths
- ✧ Let your answer have some details
- ✧ Answers that tie to your resume build trust

People frequently drop experience off of resumes. They may be embarrassed by the job; they may think it's not relevant to current work; they may be concerned about ageism.

Don't be embarrassed about putting food on the table. Carefully weigh what you drop—if anything. Don't drop jobs that show key strengths and increasing responsibility.

Recently at a local college, I was talking to someone who worked in a hospital as a janitor. She was studying at the college for a medical assistant degree.

Like most folks that I try to help, she seemed to think her qualifications were worse than someone else's. Yet as she spoke, I was thinking: who knows better the workings of a hospital than someone working there?

Chapter 2: Interviewing

She can prove that she is dependable and maybe even have recommendations from hospital staff. Also more than others just starting in the medical field, she can claim to really understand why she chose her career direction and where she wants to work.

It also shows her work ethic and willingness to do a job, even the less desirable parts. Don't neglect your qualifications—and remember your experience can be outside your chosen career.

You would be surprised to see the kinds of experience that people throw away. I've seen military experience; work in stores or warehouses, and restaurant work thrown away.

For a variety of reasons people may discount these pieces of work. In the case of military work, frequently people can't explain it to non-military employers!

And yet many employers might value military experience greatly. If you don't value the experience, will the interviewer? And yet we all derive our most basic work experiences from these—and some of the best stories.

Not all experience is paid experience

This is especially true in cases where a person is changing careers. Unpaid volunteer experience can be valuable to show an understanding of certain careers.

I advised a young engineer who decided to work in the nonprofit sector. She worked for a time without pay, to establish a non-engineering credential. Now she works for a non-profit as an operations manager.

Make yourself memorable

This is the most entertaining advice to offer to people who may be nervous about interviewing. If you are nervous about interviewing, chances are the last thing you want to be in memorable! But, being memorable is valuable—if it's the right type of memorable.

Imagine for a moment that you are an interviewer. Chances are you are working full time, so when the need arises to hire someone you squeeze the interviews into a manageable chunk of time. Say that you interview 8 people for the job.

You want to get this all over with as quickly as possible, so you set aside Tuesday and Wednesday afternoons to interview and stack up your interviews one per hour on the hour. You take notes to keep these eight people straight in your head.

By Thursday, do you really remember what the second or third interviewee said? Hmmm, probably not. And guess who gets hired? The person that is remembered has the edge.

Chapter 2: Interviewing

How to be memorable (in a good way)
- Be prepared
- Good handshake when introduced
- Manners
- Ask about the job and interviewer
- Good handshake at end of interview with closing line "Thanks for seeing me, I think I can bring dependability to this job."
- After the interview, issue a Thank-you with same closing line

Psychologists describe two interlinked effects: primacy and recency

Primacy means that people remember the first thing they hear. *Recency* means people remember the last thing they hear. Students can test themselves on both these effects. Consider what you remember about a lecture. Do you remember the first and last things?

Interviewees can use these effects to their advantage, by making a clean, clear first impression. They can also use these effects by saying something relevant early and also late in the interview. I suggest pointing out your top quality with the initial and final handshake.

"Thanks Mr. Smith for interviewing me, I think I can really bring a fresh approach to this position."

Then, follow up in a thank-you note with the same words. Have this planned before the interview.

How do I do this?

Let's start with explaining what you know and come up with a strategy. Clearly you know where you heard about the job. Maybe a friend referred you or you read an ad. Here's a sampling from a local paper. Similarly, you could do this same analysis on postings on a job board. The type of position also doesn't matter.

Ad 1—Sign-In Bonus! Helper for Home is a large home care company with offices throughout the state, we are looking for caring RNs, LPNs, HHAs, CNAs. We serve Brownstown and surrounding areas. We offer competitive salaries, paid vacation and holidays, supplemental help, vision and dental. We have advancement opportunity and annual rate increases.

Ad 2—Total Nursing Care. Total Nursing has provided 30 + years of Home Care to the Brownstown area. Due to business growth and recent promotions our

Chapter 2: Interviewing

agency has job opportunities. We need: A Clinical Coordinator (2 yrs. home care exp.); 32 hr. LPN; 32 hr. RN; PRN positions. Be part of a Great Team!

Ad 3—Medical Assistant. Needed part-time for busy specialty office. Brownstown M-F 9-4:30. Patient Prep, Precert knowledge, scheduling, test, obtain vitals & ability to assist.

Each of these ads says something unique about the position. Some have a little unique information like geography and hours. Ironically the smallest ad (the last) has the most clues to what they are looking for. I'm not surprised: a supervisor, not an HR representative probably wrote the last ad.

If you don't find an ad interesting, it's usually because it was written by a big company. For big companies, you should find someone who works there and ask, "What are they most looking for?" but also be aware that big companies look for people who 'fit' into a corporate culture—so look for clues about that culture online or in LinkedIn.

Let's look at the small ad again. One thing that jumps out is that they are a busy office. So what does an employer want in a busy office? They want dependable people, who can be flexible and handle time pressures.

'Stories' from your past should support flexibility, dependability, problem solving in customer situations. The important thing is that you show that you understand the relevance of your experience to the current job opening. If the job requires availability to a geographic area or unusual hours then stress your flexibility.

Make your answers stress your specific qualifications. Don't try to be everything, but stress more what you offer best.

There is an old story about two guys being chased by a bear. The punch line is that you don't have to be faster than the bear—just faster than the other guy.

Interviewing is like that. You want to convey why to hire you and not the next guy through the door.

How to make an interview plan in 6 easy steps

1. Take a piece of paper; fold it in half lengthwise. On the left, write the specific top qualifications that your research says they want. Include the unique things you see in ads, things other resources have told you and your strengths, which you know, are useful in the position.

Chapter 2: Interviewing

2. On the right, write ways that you meet each of those qualifications.

3. Place a check by each that you have a 'story' for.

4. Place a second check by each of these that you can tie to your resume.

5. Place a third check by each story or answer that you have practiced.

6. Below those two columns write the contact information of the interviewer.

If you have 5-10 entries on the left and responses to each on the right with three check marks afterwards and you have the contact information then you are ready for the interview. Take this with you to the interview.

After the interview write down some notes while you remember them on the back of the sheet. Write down what you like about the job, what you don't like. Write down what worked in the interview and what you need to do better.

Plan-in-hand, you are ready if your interviewer is trained, but also if the interviewer is not trained. If he/

she simply checks the dates of your resume, they'll still be impressed. If the interviewer stumbles through the interview comparing you to himself or to others in the job, won't they still be impressed? Ask yourself: using this technique won't I do better than I would without?

A final note about interviewing

While conducting a mock interview, the prospective employee told –almost—the best interview story that I've ever heard. She talked about how she'd taken initiative the first day of a job at a newspaper and managed to save the newspaper's most important advertising client.

> *"Don't let your tongue be your worst enemy."* —John "Sonny" Franzese

The story was detailed, credible and truly showcased how she could perform under pressure and take initiative in a tough situation. Except for the fact that—every few sentences she interjected about how smart she was to see the solution and how 'stupid' her boss was for not seeing the solution.

When you are interviewing for a job, your interviewer is trying to picture you in the job. This girl just told her prospective boss that she would be quick to see that boss as 'stupid.'

If she had cleaned up the story to just tell the facts instead of her assessment of her boss' failings, she would have aced the interview. Make sure you are telling the story that you think you are.

What a trained interviewer is told

Before the interview
- ✧ Identify the needs for the position
- ✧ Identify the personal traits that match these needs
- ✧ Plan your questions

During the interview
- ✧ Create rapport
- ✧ Be alert for body language
- ✧ Listen
- ✧ Take notes
- ✧ Ask follow-up questions
- ✧ Allow interviewee to answer (be quiet!)
- ✧ Thank the interviewee

After the interview
- ✧ Look over notes highlight as needed
- ✧ Write a summary
- ✧ Reach your conclusion

What this means to you

Before the interview
- Research likely competencies for the position
- Identify your strengths
- Identify 'stories' that you can tell based on your experience that support these competencies (make sure resume matches these)
- Plan your answers
- Practice—in front of a mirror or with a friend
- Make sure you can explain any gaps in resumes

During the interview
- Relax
- Create rapport
- Listen
- Make your interest in this job apparent
- Don't worry about silence
- If the interviewer probes, respond with 'stories' that convey your key competencies and qualities

After the interview
- Shake hands, deliver closing line (with main reason why you'd be best for this job)
- Write thank-you in the car, return and deliver it to front desk or drop in mail immediately.

Chapter 2: Interviewing

"Shoot me. But I'm not going to answer any questions."
—Venero Benny
"Eggs" Mangano

Chapter 3: Negotiating Salary

An Offer I Can't Refuse

"I'll make him an offer he can't refuse."
—Don Corleone, "The Godfather"

We all read about how top executives get golden parachutes, stock options and wonderful benefit plans. What about the little guy? During salary negotiations, do you feel like you get what Marilyn Monroe's character, Sugar Kane Kowalczyk, in "Some like it Hot" called the "fuzzy end of the lollypop?"

You can successfully and pleasantly negotiate salary and terms. It starts by understanding the system. In this chapter we will teach you how to negotiate and get the best terms, as well as how to set your career up strategically to achieve more. We'll even talk about the 'magic words' of negotiation.

Do you want to be hired and get PAID more?

There are two people in the room. One is you. The other is your boss. You are nervous. Maybe the boss starts your salary discussion with some sort of performance review. He tells you that you need to improve in certain areas. You start thinking, "Here it comes! No raise!" So now you are mad.

He brings up some weeks-old conflict with a coworker, and hesitates a bit. He seems to try to be fair, but you know the full story and are getting madder and madder.

Now he pauses a moment and talks about the tough business environment. You are thinking about bills you have to pay and start figuring you aren't going to get a penny! Your jaw clenches tighter than a vice. You wish fervently that you knew a way to have a voice in pay raises.

Ahhh, but you do have a voice. And if you don't start using it, you won't get the best wage you can. There are two people in the room—you are there too! Use your voice effectively. You do this by using some simple strategies. We'll start by understanding how the boss thinks. Here's his story:

He came into the room almost as nervous as you. A week ago he was told by his boss what your raise would be; his boss was told by Human Resources. Maybe he was told a range of raises and given a small amount of latitude—maybe not.

He built up the courage to talk to you for a few days. He's behind in his work, so he decides—stupidly—to combine that performance review that he owes you

Chapter 3: Negotiating Salary

with the raise discussion. He's not thinking this will make you angry. But nobody told him how to manage.

He wishes he knew what you do all day. He may either guiltily realize that he doesn't know your job, or arrogantly think he does and that you are less efficient than he would be.

He really wishes he knew how to best handle these discussions. He really wishes he knew how to convince his boss to give his team better raises—and he resents that he won't get a decent raise either.

He's human so he's torn between the better and worse angels of his nature. The selfish part of him wants to be sure that he gets a better raise than you—and he knows he can't control that by raising his salary—only by lowering yours.

But he also may be afraid that people will leave, either because someone else gets a better raise or because nobody gets a raise. Wow! What can you do with that?

Who knew that your boss might not be the one setting your raise? Who knew that it may have been handed to him?

Now, a particularly frustrating thought occurs to you: If he isn't the guy with the power and you talk to him, not the guys in power, what exactly can you do by talking to him. So even if you come up with the magic words, can he do much to help you?

Tip 1—Know what the boss can do

He can probably work within boundaries set for him. If he was given a range of raises, you may be able to wiggle a little more for you. He may also be able to do other things—approve a more flexible schedule that allows you to waste less gas in traffic or avoid a babysitter. He may be able to pay part of your college/training. He may also be able to approve you trying other types of work.

> *"Honest people have no ethics."*
> *—Sam DeCavalcante*

If you want to do the website for your team, because that builds skills for you. He may be able to help get you that assignment

In most cases salary ranges are set by Human Resource departments in big companies, or approved above your supervisor's level. This is partly to ensure consistency and partly to keep low-level managers from giving away the store to look like the 'good boss.'

How do companies decide salary?

A company wants to have good enough salaries to get and keep good employees, but low enough salaries

Chapter 3: Negotiating Salary

to retain a healthy profit. Big companies need a process to determine salary that appears 'fair and equitable.' This is an important legal phrase.

In short, no company wants to be sued because of bias of any kind in their salaries paid. So how can they determine a fair wage?

Most people would consider a wage fair if that wage were similar to what was paid for similar experience level, similar work in a similar geographic area. You can find the wage ranges on several wage sites online. Take a look at Salary.com.

Let's pretend you are an Accountant working in Financial Services, in Boston, MA.

If I search on Salary.com for Accountant salaries in Boston, MA, I find that an Accountant II makes $59,000. An Accountant III makes $71,000. That's an $11,000 difference.

What's really interesting is that there isn't much difference between an Accountant II and an Accountant III. Here are the descriptions:

Accountant II—Prepares balance sheets, profit and loss statements, and other financial reports. Responsibilities also include analyzing trends, costs, revenues, financial commitments, and obligations incurred to predict future revenues and expenses. Reports organization's finances to management, and offers suggestions about resource utilization, tax strategies, and assumptions underlying budget forecasts. <u>May require a bachelor's degree in area of specialty and 2-4 years of experience in the field or in a related area. Familiar with standard concepts, practices, and procedures within a particular field. Relies on experience and judgment to plan and accomplish goals. Performs a variety of tasks. Works under general supervision. A certain degree of creativity and latitude is required. Typically reports to a supervisor or manager.</u>

Accountant III—Prepares balance sheets, profit and loss statements, and other financial reports. Responsibilities also include analyzing trends, costs, revenues, financial commitments, and obligations incurred to predict future revenues and expenses. Reports organization's finances to management, and offers suggestions about resource utili-

Chapter 3: Negotiating Salary

zation, tax strategies, and assumptions underlying budget forecasts. <u>Requires a bachelor's degree in area of specialty, and 4-6 years of experience in the field or in a related area. Familiar with a variety of the field's concepts, practices, and procedures. Relies on experience and judgment to plan and accomplish goals. Performs a variety of complicated tasks. May lead and direct the work of others. A wide degree of creativity and latitude is expected. Typically reports to a manager or head of a unit/ department.</u> [1]

Notice that the descriptions are very similar. Only the underlined text is different. Many of the differences may be subjective.

Try looking up salaries online for your job title. You can find similar results for many different job titles.

Hmmm, I wonder how many people are classified as Accountant II, but are really doing Accountant III work? Or how many accountants have worked more than four years in their field and never realized

---

[1] Source: salary.com

that they have passed a milestone? That's an instant $11,000 question!

Tip 2—Know how your job is classified

More importantly, if you properly arm him, your boss can argue for your higher salary—if you can prove that you are misclassified. Show him these classifications and he may want to take this up-the-line.

The moral of the story is that salary classification is your strongest negotiation card. Time on the job, education, experiences, type of work can move you from Accountant II to Accountant III—and get you 11K more.

Tip 3—Be prepared to support why people like you get paid more—and choose your data carefully

Be aware that salaries in San Diego aren't the same as those for the same job in San Francisco. In some cities suburbs may have different salaries than the cities they neighbor.

Small shifts in geography can mean thousands of dollars. If you do a search for northern Illinois, also do a search for Chicago.

Chapter 3: Negotiating Salary

Tip 4—Your boss might not be able to change your pay rate, but still can increase your hours or save you money

These are tough times. When aren't they? But even tough times do offer opportunities. You have to look for them. And given the job market, look for them where you are if possible.

EXAMPLE: If you are part-time working 20 hours a week, and they look to hire a second person part-time, see if you can convince them that one fulltime (you) is a better deal. What do you get? Benefits, more hours.

EXAMPLE: If your boss changes your hours at your request, you may be able to reduce commute costs or childcare costs.

Tip 5—Talk your boss into changing your job title. Look for your own strategic advantage three years from now

Use today's tough times to strategically build experience. When the job market loosens, you will be qualified for more money. Your boss might be surprised to have you ask for a certain assignment, but you'll know that getting this assignment can make your argument that you fit a higher paid classification better next year.

In the example above, asking for an assignment that allows for "A wide degree of creativity and latitude" may be the last item that prevents you from receiving that $11,000 raise.

Look for these opportunities several years out and consider asking for them in advance. You can imply an agreement that if you take on certain tasks that in a year or so you will qualify for a raise.

Tip 6—Use the magic words

Since companies are sensitive to the words "fair and equitable," you should use them without implying any threat of legal action. State that you only want a fair wage and want to be fairly treated.

Then use the statistics to show what you think is fair, giving your boss a copy of the printout. By doing this you may be able to shift the negotiations to your grounds.

Of course, you should expect that HR probably has a similar printout citing the lower position's range of pay. You'd like to shift your boss's perception to accept your data.

If your boss can respond he will. If not he may pass the information on to someone who can alter

Chapter 3: Negotiating Salary

your next pay discussion. You may just see the entry in your paycheck citing an 'equity adjustment'—as I did. Don't hesitate to use these words multiple times in the discussion—always carefully and without threat.

Tip 7—Position yourself at the bottom of a higher range of salaries

I've simplified above and talked about one salary figure. In reality the salaries are stated in ranges. The salary range for Accountant II may overlap with the salary range for Accountant III. Normally you want to be considered at the bottom of the higher range rather than at the top of the lower range.

This allows you room for growth and makes it more likely for a company to raise your wages in subsequent years. It's a smart trade to consider getting the title changed even if your current wage doesn't change.

Tip 8—If possible put more than money on the table

Negotiations are easiest to accomplish if you are negotiating on more than one thing. Aside from money, consider putting benefits on the table, time off or future opportunities.

If your boss can't give you money, he may be willing to give you something else that may be of value to you.

This is a classic negotiations technique that allows both parties to 'win' (We talk more about win-win negotiations later in this book)

Finally, close your negotiation on a good note, with a reminder how much you enjoy bringing value to the job. If possible cite a specific item or two which you bring to the job.

Remember that you are not only a specialist, but the right specialist! You want your boss to be glad you are continuing in your position.

Tip 9—When in doubt, ask anyway! And ask in several ways!

Studies have shown that many people don't like negotiating. Not surprisingly people learn to avoid what they dislike. They simply accept terms offered. I understand. (Even though I'm sure the tough guys would call me a wimp!)

I've avoided such unpleasant things as calling credit card companies, calling telephone companies, calling vendors who have raised prices.

Pay particular attention to how salary and raises are apportioned. Before the final discussion—months before a raise discussion, and in a hiring discussion sometime before the offer—ask pointed questions

Chapter 3: Negotiating Salary

about how exactly raises, benefits and salaries are decided.

Be pleasant, but be informed. Ask if there is 'any way' to do better the next time the evaluation is made. Then thank them with a smile.

Tip 10—If you can't ask, at least inform and wait

A young woman was put in an unusual position, because she was moved from an hourly job to a salaried job with no overtime, her promotion cost her money. She felt very frustrated because the lost overtime was the money that she was using to pay off a college debt. She explained the situation to her boss. She didn't ask, beg or demand. She just explained and made him aware of her problem. While her boss was not in a position to pay her more immediately, he was impressed with her job performance and honesty. He surprised her with a $7000 raise in 3 months. That amount more than made up for her lost overtime.

Other applications of negotiations

I knew people who could whine and get discounts on products, services or higher pay—anything! I felt I couldn't do that. I'm just not a demander, or whiner.

I'm an asker. So I was ready to give up in advance of any discussion.

Then I found out that it's not the demanding the whining or even a superior asking techniques that get results. It just involves asking and not giving up. I could stay true to my character and remain polite.

I could simply ask, "What else can be done for me?" Then be quiet for a bit. This is the hard part. See if the guy on the other end of the table or telephone says anything. If he hesitates, ask the question another way, "What would you ask for?" or "What else can you do for me?" Frequently, other items might be added to sweeten a deal.

Once I learned what I was missing, I learned to ask, and ask, and ask. Here are a few times I've asked and gotten more than I expected.

- When in the process of getting hired by a local company, I asked for a signing bonus. My argument? If they hired another non-local engineer they would need to pay relocation costs. I asked for that same amount as a signing bonus. I was surprised that the manager agreed! This cash came in handy, as cash always does. Studies have shown that women in technical fields rarely if ever try to haggle over their pay. This fact alone probably accounts for much of the pay differential.

Chapter 3: Negotiating Salary

✧ As a small business owner I avoided the FedEx 'salesperson' when she called. I was always too busy. One day I picked up the phone, to my complete surprise she immediately offered my company a higher discount on shipping—much higher. From then on forward, I took her calls always discussing new business and then asking what else FedEx could do for us. Several salespeople later, I'm continually surprised what gets offered. Keep in mind this is all legal, and moral. I was offered these discounts to grow my business. When my business grows I ship more and more with FedEx. They like helping me grow.

✧ Similarly, my company has an 800 number, because we make and receive a large volume of long distance calls. Now that the FedEx salesperson had already 'taught' me, I started asking for more and more discounts. Now I call the telephone people periodically and ask what further discounts they can give me. One time they basically told me the 'best' rates that the big companies get—and how to get them as a small company. I was shocked that they offered this inside information!

✧ In my business we process credit cards. We pay a company to process them for MasterCard, Visa,

Discover and Amex. I started calling every six months and asking for them for further discounts. I was surprised how normal this conversation was for them.

- In a recent 30-minute phone call to a supplier, I saved $ 95 per month. If you figure that was for 6 months. That's $570 for a half hour. And the phone call wasn't that unpleasant.

- You can even apply this to hotels. Ask for upgrades at check-in. Try: "Would it be possible to…" as a start to your request. It won't always work, but it sometimes will.

- You can make this easy for yourself by being pleasant. Call a vendor and ask for an audit of your account. Ask if they have any special discounts that you aren't currently getting. Ask in SEVERAL different ways. "Is there anything else that I should be doing?" and "Is there anything that I am missing?"

Watching and learning from public negotiations

You can see some of these techniques in public situations. The more you look for them, the more you

Chapter 3: Negotiating Salary

will see them. As you see negotiations techniques in use, try to learn from them.

Part I: Congress

You can see a peek behind the scenes and see negotiations at work by following political news. A recent discussion on Immigration Reform pitted one party against the other.

Remember that discussions on this topic have been ongoing for decades. In fact, each party has claimed victory several times and agreements have been reached and signed. Oddly enough a few years later the need for reform re-occurs.

Recently, one side argued to take part of the issue and write smaller bills addressing each of these parts. The suggestion was that immigration for agriculture might be separated from immigration of technical workers. And that border control enforcement could be a third separate bill.

The second party instantly objected. They wanted all issues considered at once in 'Comprehensive Reform.' My guess is that this party is protecting a core issue by making sure that multiple items remain on the table. That way they can ensure that they trade away items that are less important to them, while protecting the one that is most important to them.

Part II: Union negotiations

Take any union/management negotiation over the last several decades. Try to find one negotiation where only wages were on the table. The main point of negotiation will almost certainly be wages, but there will be several other points raised: work conditions, hours, vacation, seniority protection, benefits, and retirement.

Union representatives have mastered the rule of putting several items on the table. Undoubtedly sympathy will be raised based on the other points, but ultimately the monetary benefits appear to be the point.

"If you have a lot of what people want and can't get, then you can supply the demand and shovel in the dough."
—Charlie "Lucky" Luciano

Chapter 4: The Value-Added Employee

Goodfellas

"You are so goddamn smart. Except you ain't."
—Eddie Dane, "Miller's Crossing"

Is your boss an enigma? Do you feel like the magic decoder ring was missing from your cracker-jack box? If you had a career coach…ah, yes, then life would be easy. But how can you get what you need to from job assignments—while being all-you-can-be to your mystifying boss? First, I'll demystify your boss, and then we'll teach you what you need to know in order to better enjoy your work.

Joan was a friend of mine. She was an administrative assistant to a group that I worked with. Her job was stressful and frankly she outclassed the work she did, but she had an event in her career that caused her to lose seniority within her union. It was one of those freak events that happens in a career. Her division was spun off, then repurchased.

She always worked for the same folks, but technically not the same company. Several years later she was the admin to one of the top executives of a large company—by his request, as I understand it—a few rules seemed to have been bent. Her reputation was rightly the best admin in the company. In private at lunch one day she reminisced about the job that was her favorite.

It was a job she held years before when she was just starting out. She didn't feel stressed at all in that job. She worked for a group of young architects. She worked very hard, but looked forward to going to work every day. It was a playful, adventurous atmosphere, where she was valued and she felt fulfilled. I'm not sure she ever recaptured that feeling within her subsequent jobs—she clearly looked back upon it wistfully at the time that she talked to me.

Have you have had more than one job? Was one better than the other? Don't you do your best work when you feel valued? Aren't you happiest when you are doing a good job—when people let you do your best? But many of us get locked into jobs where nobody seems to understand the linkage between doing your best work—and the freedom to do your best work.

You can be the minimum, or you can be the average or you can be better than average. Clearly being the minimum puts you at risk for firing or at least poor future prospects. Being average won't get you advancement or raises. Being better than average gains you advantages.

Chapter 4: The Value-Added Employee

I don't say be the best because being the best has risks. While those risks can be managed it's not for the faint-hearted. Besides being the best can start turf wars and frankly is a matter of opinion. But primarily it simply triggers the wrong type of competition. It's absolutely fine being the best employee that you can be, just don't pursue recognition beyond all else.

Some might say that what I call the *Value-Added Employee* is another way of saying being what your employer might say is 'ideal.' The 'Value-Added Employee' means to me: a type of employee who adds value to the team, the company, the product and themselves. Here's a list that draws a line between average and value-added:

AVERAGE

- ✧ Does what they are told
- ✧ Is trainable
- ✧ Gets along with others
- ✧ Speaks only when spoken to
- ✧ Communicates unimportant information
- ✧ Reacts to problems
- ✧ Pleasant
- ✧ Won't take responsibility
- ✧ Makes promises, some realistic
- ✧ Impacted by home at work—likely stressed at home
- ✧ Thinks of job

VALUE-ADDED

- ✧ Thinks ahead
- ✧ Trains others—or mentors others
- ✧ Self improves, self-educates
- ✧ Keeps the peace
- ✧ Communicates important information
- ✧ Anticipates, prevents problems
- ✧ Values other people; a person others want to work with
- ✧ Owns their own actions
- ✧ Does what they say, says what they'll do
- ✧ Leaves work at work, leaves home at home
- ✧ Thinks team, not self

When you look at these lists, most of the behaviors in the first are not bad behaviors. None are likely to get an employee fired. Most wouldn't be mentioned in a job review as problems. Most would never be mentioned to the employee as holding them back in their career development.

Many of these behaviors may even be stated by your boss as desirable! Only a career coach would notice these or advise an employee to change these behaviors—or would they? Are you likely to hire an executive career coach? Naw, me neither. And yet, when you see the first list next to the second list you can see the difference.

Chapter 4: The Value-Added Employee

Would you be surprised that the second set of behaviors can earn you more money? There's a catch, but they can. The catch is that people must see these things about you clearly. Most of these differences could also be seen as 'emotional intelligence' or maturity. Further, they are characteristics of happy, satisfied and successful people.

Finally, notice that Behavioral Interview Questions are based on these behaviors. In essence you've prepared for these questions in interviews, so it shouldn't surprise you that people really want these traits in their best employees. It shouldn't surprise you that people who can consistently show these traits are more easily hired, more easily promoted and more highly valued at work. So once hired it's time to walk the walk, not just talk the talk, because you do want to retain the job too!

Behavioral interview questions

Have you interviewed lately? Chances are you have been asked, or have prepared to be asked one of those 'open-ended' questions like: "Where do you see yourself in 5 years?" or "Tell me about a challenge you faced on the job" or "Tell me about a time when you had a conflict with a co-worker." Or "Tell me what you see as your biggest weakness?" These open-ended questions are intended to get you talking about how you actually behave at work. They are supposed to answer: "How will you handle a real world situation?"

Oddly enough people now prepare their answers so carefully (providing canned answers that provide as little information as possible) for these questions that they frequently defeat the purpose of them!

How should you answer these questions? You should see them as an opportunity. Realize that you are being asked how you will handle a situation in the new job.

Using an example from your resume will builds credibility, "When I worked at ABC Corp…" tell a true story that illustrates that you can react with maturity and learn from a tough situation. No matter what the exact question, the only real question you are answering is why they should hire you, not the next guy through the door.

How to change? How to cultivate these behaviors?

How you think is everything

Review the behaviors, really read them. Make sure you see the benefits of the behavior. If you really believe that these are better you will automatically incorporate them in your life.

Chapter 4: The Value-Added Employee

Consider a sports metaphor. Imagine Lin from the Knicks. This guy was in the news a few years back for transforming his team. Yet, he has always credited them, right? Do you get the feeling this guy is pleasant to work with? Passes the ball, right? Thinks ahead? You've heard that throughout his life he self-improved. If Lin can do this, can you?

Build relationships from day one

First see everyone as someone, then as someone you can build a relationship with.

Understand viewpoints; remain helpful and supportive. Never gossip: gossiping decreases trust. People will always assume you will talk about them.

"No bum talks about a bum."
—Carlo Gambino

See yourself as someone who can solve problems and help people

Don't worry if you encounter an agenda, just don't buy into it. If ever you encounter a difficult personality, one way to cope with that person is to consider what you respect about them. The trait you respect will be what you later remember about them. You can deal with a person you see as passionate better than one you see as obstinate.

> *"One hand washes the other…both hands wash the face."* —*Sam Giancana*

Communicate

Tie your behavior to these behaviors.

EXAMPLE: "Thinking ahead, I think we can prevent some problems if we…" This doesn't mean bragging. It means being clear what your motives are.

Improvement starts with you

It's tempting to find fault with others. It's easier to fault others than it is to fix yourself. But the reality is that you ONLY control YOU. In tough situations, consider how you can react better. Think how you can influence events.

Find role models

One of the most powerful things I've ever done was to write down a list of people that I admire and why. I found some strange things out.

First, I admired a lot of people. Second, the reasons I admired them were vastly different—and reflected my personal values.

I also learned how to express that admiration to them. In fact I made a point of it. In some cases I

Chapter 4: The Value-Added Employee

returned to them for advice. It was easier to ask when they knew why I was asking for their advice.

EXAMPLE: "I've always admired how you can handle tough situations with co-workers." Later, I'd be able to ask advice about handling such situations. Notice that this approach also indicates that you value other people, anticipate and prevent problems.

Collect your own stories

One of the strongest sets of experiences to learn from are your own—both good and bad. But your friends also provide stories to learn from. The stories in this book, generally detail positive experiences from friends and colleagues.

How to benefit?

"The relation between emotional intelligence, assessed with a performance measure, and positive workplace outcomes was examined in 44 analysts and clerical employees from the finance department of a Fortune 400 insurance company. Emotionally intelligent individuals received greater merit increases and held higher company rank than their counterparts. They also received better peer and/or supervisor ratings of

interpersonal facilitation and stress tolerance than their counterparts."[1]

"Employee happiness has long been linked to better job performance. Now, research suggests that happiness is linked to a quantifiable attribute known as "emotional intelligence."[2]

I considered using the word 'profit' instead of 'benefit,' but the benefits go beyond profit. If you consider the people that you know who fit the category of value-added employees or emotionally intelligent people, you quickly realize that they seem a bit charmed. They tend to work hard, but be successful. They tend to have more fulfilling, enriched lives and they are happier.

The main benefit is that satisfaction. It makes sense. If you think more of the team, rather than self, you are less selfish. Being less selfish tends to mean being more happy. The person who is a peacemaker tends to be at personal peace. Again he seems happier.

---

[1] Psicothema, ISSN EDICIÓN EN PAPEL: 0214-9915, 2006. Vol. 18, Suplem.1, pp. 132-138

[2] http://www.businessnewsdaily.com/222-emotional-intelligence-increases-employee-happiness.html

Chapter 4: The Value-Added Employee

The person preventing problems, not reacting to problems is usually less stressed. Again, he's happier. I'd rather be the dog wagging the tail rather than the tail, wouldn't you?

And studies have shown a strong correlation between people feeling a sense of control over their lives and a feeling of happiness. Ask yourself, once you decided on a career, wasn't that when you started to feel happier?

Now, about that other word "profit." Obviously the better employee tends to get better opportunities. If you've collected the stories of your work life you can justify better qualifications—and more responsibility, more maturity lead to more pay.

> *"You will put the garbage in the cans and make certain that the cans are covered. We got to keep our own backyard clean."* —John Gotti

You could silently implement these things and hope someone notices, but a stronger approach it to simply make clear that these behaviors are a priority to you.

In short talk about them. "I'm making an effort to think about the team here" (when you are).

Or tell a coworker that you value them. Remember that you don't need to get to all this immediately.

Implementing just one or two behaviors is a start. And you can choose which.

I divide emotional intelligence into three interlocking areas. Think of them as interlocking gears:

Preparation, communication, and people

You could build strength in any one of these skill areas and you'd improve your emotional intelligence.

Preparation
- Improve yourself
- Improve others—connect them to resources
- Gauge impact on others; predict the team dynamics

People
- Have friends in low places (and high places)
- Don't just network; build relationship Value the contributions of others
- Remember it's never just about you. You control only your actions and reactions, but these are powerful shapers of your world.

Communication
- Think before you speak
- Make comments non-personal; don't gossip
- Make sure you clearly state the important information

Chapter 4: The Value-Added Employee

- ✧ Tie communications to your core values
- ✧ Listen more than you talk

At the beginning of this chapter, I told you a story of an administrative assistant named Joan. What really made her ideal job so great? While Joan certainly couldn't recreate that entire environment, she can improve the current one and she did.

"Boy, you know every time I see Hole-in-the-Wall again, it's like seeing it fresh for the first time. And every time that happens, I keep asking myself the same question: how could I be so damn stupid to keep coming back here?"
—Butch Cassidy, "Butch Cassidy & the Sundance Kid"

Emotional intelligence can provide some of the solutions. Joan felt it was her ideal job, but I'd guess that this same environment benefitted the others who worked there. Her bosses and other employees clearly felt relaxed and productive.

In an ideal job, bosses and employees are mostly on the same side. And all benefit from reduced stress, happier environments, and more productive environments—this is yet another way of saying that all parties benefit from emotional intelligence.

Joan did manage to find a position she preferred. She moved within the company to another very valuable position.

She felt valued last time we talked. And 'yes' even in that conversation she talked about that one job—the one years ago—that got away. She still seemed wistful to me.

Butch Cassidy: [singing]

*"Don't ever hit your mother with a shovel.
It will leave a dull impression
on her mind."*

*—"Butch Cassidy & the
Sundance Kid"*

Chapter 5: Conflict Resolution

You Talking to Me?

"Now I know why tigers eat their young."
—Al Capone

Conflict is part of life. How can you de-stress conflicts and make your work environment and your home environment—if not perfect—a lot easier to deal with? As Max Lucade once said, "Conflict is inevitable, but combat is optional."

How can you 'fix' conflicts and de-escalate combat to a manageable conflict? While nobody can live a life without conflict, you can manage the stress involved and reduce the level of conflict.

If you want a simple metaphor for conflict resolution, considers the relationship between parents and teenagers. Have you ever listened to a conversation between a parent and a teen?

That's poor communication. As society changes, can anyone doubt there exists a set of different values, beliefs, and attitudes between two generations?

As a child moves through the treacherous waters before reaching adulthood aren't there discrepancies in expectations? And of course there is a history of prior conflicts.

If ever there were a recipe for conflict it would include these same elements: poor communication, different values & beliefs, discrepancies in expectations and a history of past conflicts.

The relationship between parent and teenager is a *firestorm*. It is the 'ideal' conflict. And anyone will understand it because we've all lived through it as we grew up. Those of us who have parented have seen this quintessential conflict from the other side too.

The parent-teen paradigm has one more lesson to impart. No matter how tough the subject of the conflict is, both sides have a very good reason to want to end up in a good place.

Ideally both sides benefit from the survival of the relationship. That's good and important, long-term relationships allow for *win-win* solutions.

Win-win solutions are ones in which both sides feel they have gotten something valuable out of the solution. Whereas *win-lose* solutions are one in which one person feels they are the 'winner' and have beaten the other side.

Typically win-lose is how most people would view negotiations with a used car salesman. Most would suspect at the end of this negotiation that they paid too much.

Chapter 5: Conflict Resolution

We've all known people who have to win or dominate at all costs. The funny thing is that nobody wants to deal with them again.

And oddly enough, that makes the 'loser' do things like seek revenge or try to even things up later. In an employment situation this can show up as a work slowdown, theft or sabotage. In a parent-teen situation this can lead to lies, deception, partial truths or worse.

We'll discuss win-win and win-lose in more detail in the next chapter. For now it's enough to remember that if you value a relationship, that you want the relationship to last.

If you want the relationship to last, then you should shift your focus to long-term results. Thus, you should strive to make sure that both parties feel good about the outcomes of all interactions.

In long-term relationships, conflicts are normal—neither good nor bad. Conflict is complex and can involve elements of past conflicts, future conflicts and present elements outside your control. You can see how all of this is true of parents and teens. Conflicts cause stress. Ongoing conflicts create misery.

The key to handling long-term relationships is to build a sense of security and trust. You want the relationship to be relaxed, include some humor, and to be focused on the 'right' things.

Who takes out the garbage ought not to result in divorce. Where an employee's desk faces shouldn't result in that employee quitting. A dispute over a parking space shouldn't result in the loss of a tenant.

To keep the focus long-term you have to handle the immediate and the mid-term issues. First, eliminate any safety, monetary and legal issues. So your first actions should be to handle the immediate issues:

> *"It's not safe to argue while driving, so let's talk about this at home."*

This also eliminates distractions. When you've gotten past the initial concerns, look to take the emotion out of issues—de-escalate them. The key to this is to be the 'bigger person' and not take offense. Restate issues without the emotion.

> *"So the problem is that you feel you don't have complete freedom."*

In the real world, this will inevitably result in an inflammatory statement blaming you. You must de-escalate again, but continually stating the problem in simple clear non-accusatory terms.

The point here is to listen—really listen. Keep eye contact and your calm. Once the other person stops escalating and agrees to your statement of the problem, you shift your focus to,

> *"Now that we clearly see the problem, let's see what we can think of to solve it in a way that we both can live with."*

Tip 1—If you can't de-escalate, then delay

Tell the other person you need time to cool down and carefully consider the problem. If they persist, schedule a time to talk about it. In a marriage that might be after the kids are in bed.

Tip 2—Be aware of personal and physical space

It's impossible to de-escalate situations if a subtle threat is sensed. Invasion of personal space is a subtle threat.

Tip 3—Communicate assertively

If you take charge, you can direct the solution. Recognize the feelings behind the words. Let's look again at the previous example:

> *"I can see that a lack of freedom could be frustrating."*

Here is a way to phrase the same concept while directing the solution:

"I can see that friction in the workplace would stress anyone. Let's see what we can do about making it easier."

Notice that handling conflicts successfully has a structure and a flavor. The flavor includes a feeling of fairness to all. The structure follows:

- Listen
- State the problem
- Reflect back your perception of the problem and its effects on each party
- Get agreement
- Set boundaries of behavior allowed in this discussion
- Seek Solutions
- Stay on task
- Reaffirm that the solution solves everyone's problem

What would change the culture of crisis?

The most frustrating situations are ones that repeat. In many families and in many workplaces and in many social environments, there exists a culture of crisis.

Chapter 5: Conflict Resolution

Much like the 'reality shows' that we try not to watch, this conflict seems to only perpetuate more conflicts.

It's a culture dominated by emotion, betrayal, and a series of hurts—real and imagined—that stretch back a generation or more. It's the Hatfields and McCoys of modern life.

> *"Whenever you're in conflict with someone, there is one factor that can make the difference between damaging your relationship and deepening it. That factor is attitude."*
> *—William James* [1]

How to change a situation that is mired in self-pity and wrongs? It's not easy and it will take time and consistency. It's easiest to see how to change this culture if you examine the techniques people use to propagate a constant feeling of crisis.

Tip 4—Emotional people up the drama, so you need to reduce daily drama

Keep your cool. Set boundaries. If someone tries to make an issue into a crisis, slow them down, have

---

[1] Leader of pragmatism, a philosophical movement that began in the 19th century—not a gangster

them think out alternative and evaluate choices. Then remember to control your response to their behavior. You may not be able to control their behavior, but you do own your own response.

> *"The greatest conflicts are not between two people but between one person and himself." —Garth Brooks* [2]

Tip 5—Difficult people might try to keep reminding you of old conflicts, so you should break those connections between events

You can't fix the past, but you can alter the future. If they connect the past and the present, remind them of the current issue and transition into problem-solving mode.

Long ago on a troubled project my team was forced to report to a group of managers. "Bill," a manager with decades of experience on the team, would inevitably start talking about problems on the team from 5, 10 and, even 15 years before. Needless to say, this had all the effect of throwing gasoline on an engine fire. I'd bring the meeting back to Earth by reminding

---

[2] A country music artist, not a gangster!

Bill gently that we had a current problem that had a current solution.

"According to my best recollection, I don't remember."
—Vincent "Jimmy Blue Eyes" Alo

TIP 6—FIND THE POSITIVE IN EVEN THE MOST CHRONICALLY DIFFICULT PEOPLE

In the case of Bill in the example above, I'd remind myself that at least he knew the history. Then I'd try to find some positive history to ask him about in the future.

TIP 7—AVOID THE BLAME GAME

If they try to attach blame to you, respond neutrally and rephrase the issue.

"So, the problem is that we are missing a deadline, right? I can add to that, part of the issue is that we are also missing some supplies we need. If we can agree that these are the two important points, we can get to a solution."

Don't place blame back on them. Be polite. Diplomacy has saved nations!

Tip 8—Avoiding power struggles

If you find yourself in a power struggle, work to change the dynamic. I was working with the resident manager of an apartment building, which I owned. She reported that two tenants were having a feud over parking. One tenant owned a subcompact car and parked in the garage. The other owned a large American made car and parked just outside the garage. The fighting involved the larger car blocking the exit of the smaller car. The resident manager believed that we'd lose one of these tenants and so did I. We didn't.

> *"Those who know when to fight and when not to fight are victorious."* —Sun Tzu [3]

My husband borrowed a paintbrush and some paint and painted the outlines of a parking place on the black top. Just a little paint changed the dynamic. Next he brought the tenant with the larger car out and showed him 'his' parking space. Of course he agreed that he could park in his 'new' space.

Next my husband brought out the owner of the compact car. Of course he agreed that he was a good enough driver to navigate out past the new

---

[3] Chinese general and author, b.500 BC—also not a gangster!

Chapter 5: Conflict Resolution

parking space. It's amazing how much defining a space can change a problem.

"A good manager doesn't try to eliminate conflict; he tries to keep it from wasting the energies of his people. If you're the boss and your people fight you openly when they think that you are wrong—that's healthy."
—Robert Townsend [4]

Tip 9—Keep a sense of humor

If you can incorporate some humor, you can frequently humanize people. This frequently will allow them to forgive each other. Forgiveness for you. Forgiveness for them. Ahhh, peace for the moment.

"Let him go. He cheated me fair & square"
—Joseph "Joe Batters" Accardo

---

[4] Also not a gangster!

Chapter 6: Tough Situations

Forgettaboutit

"You wouldn't kill me in cold blood, would ya?"
—Roy Parker

"No, I'll let ya warm up a little."
—Cody Jarrett

—"White Heat"

Customers and others are sometimes impossible to deal with. And yet, some people seem to be able to handle the toughest customers without breaking a sweat. What do they know that you wish you knew? Their skills go beyond conflict management, and extend to really tough areas. If you learn what they know, you can move these tough customers from partners in conflict to pussycats that purr with relief and gratitude.

In the last chapter, we talked about long-term relationships. In this chapter we talk about tough situations. Tough situations tend to be situations where the relationship is valuable, but you haven't yet had the opportunity to build a report and strength in the relationship. This isn't typical of a parent-teen relationship, but is more similar to dealing with a complaining customer. Sometimes at work, you encounter people who make simple interactions difficult. You may not care to make these folks your mentor, or friend: your goal may be simple coexistence. Or maybe you crave just the ability to deal with a coworker or a complaining customer.

Why do companies care?

In the case of a customer, your boss will care. The reason is simply that unhappy customers share negative experiences with others for approximately 18 months. Future sales get lost.

Even worse, unhappy customers often make the employees unhappy, which can lead to high employee turnover. Unhappy employees tend to result in unhappy customers—it becomes a cycle.

On the other hand, really good managers understand that customer complaints can lead to better product and stronger customer loyalty—if handled well. 95% of unhappy customers will remain loyal if their complaint is handled well.[1]

---

[1] Source: Lee Resource, Inc.

Chapter 6: Tough Situations

In the case of impossible co-workers—if you have difficulty dealing with this person, it's likely that your work and their work are *both* impacted by the situation.

Worse still, it's likely that few others can easily deal with this person. You have the opportunity to make a whole group more productive.

Why do you care?

Handling these 'tough customers' is a valuable soft-skill that leads to more responsibility and more pay. You can reduce your own stress—and coworker stress. And you frequently can be the good guy; it feels *good* to be the good guy.

A smart employee realizes that the same customer handling techniques work in co-worker relations—and employee-boss relations (and in marriages and families at times).

Four things need to be mentioned

✧ If a situation becomes a true threat to you or someone else, you must follow safety procedures.

✧ If a situation is a legal situation, you must defer to the legal experts.

- ✧ If a situation involves something beyond your control or authority, escalate it appropriately.

- ✧ You can't negotiate with someone who isn't willing to be honest.

Here are a few simple ideas of how to get easy stress-free results. This chapter has three parts—in the first part, we talk about types of things anyone can do; in the second, we talk about what works for different people; in the third we talk about negotiating.

Part I: Steps anyone can take

1—Quick action. Time pressures make people act erratically. When a customer has a complaint they feel enormous pressure to get an answer quickly.

Research has shown that people with complaints act like people in pain. People in pain lash out, become defensive and don't behave logically. Customers lash out and become defensive.

2—Enhance feeling of "I've found the right person" and your reliability. Promise little steps and deliver quickly.

"Right now I'm going to call Fed Ex and find out where your package is."

Chapter 6: Tough Situations

Make guilt-free cost-free good-faith offers:

"Would you like the tracking number?"

I was recently in a chamber session with a top Marketing/PR guy. He made the point that sales have much to do with trust, as does Public Relations. When rehabilitating a firm's image after major issues (think BP and gulf spill) his team recommends that the company think of the first three small steps they should take.

Next, they take those steps and make certain that the steps have been accomplished—but before they even mention them, and immediately after announcing them—they announce the completion of their goals "early." This technique allows the company to rebuild trust and its public image.

Whenever possible don't lead with 'No.' Try to talk about what you can do, and explain why. You want to be as proactive as possible, and make sure that the customer sees that.

3—Listening/answering thinking. It's natural to go on the defensive. But even comments like "that service isn't included in our price" or denying that there is a problem will simply make a customer more anxious and angry.

Instead, your first answer may be non-committal like "Hmmm" or "OK, let's hear more," or "I'd like to hear what happened from the beginning." This does several things. First, it focused the customer on recalling, not being angry. This allows them to vent as well as to fully describe the problem. Oddly enough many angry customers will vent as you listen—and then apologize to you for complaining.

Those that don't, will have listed all of their issues. Frequently, you can fix a few of the issues easily and they will drop the rest.

I had a major customer problem. When this customer called, they were angry. I went a few steps further from this technique and said what a normal customer rep could not…I said, "You are right. I didn't like the resulting product either, but I had to work under the deadline agreed to. Now what can we do to make this right?" The fellow was stunned.

He actually went on to agree that not all the problems were attributable to my product. He also gave me an extension of time to work on it.

I kept him updated, delivered a product he liked… and got a glowing thank-you from him…in which he stated that he'd never had a company provide such customer service.

If I had not resolved this issue, I'd have had to refund a major order. This customer would never had ordered again. He'd have told others not to order from me. The cost from the original order alone would have been about $4000. I didn't get off scot free, but the cost out of pocket was about $2000. And we learned to produce a much better product. Plus we have a customer who will order again and recommend us.

4—Problem/solution thinking. Shift the customer's thinking about a problem by making sure you shift talk away from blame for the past and toward "what we can fix,"

> *"What could we do today that might make you happy?" "I just want to be fair to everyone, can you think of a fair solution to this?"*

If the problem is delivery, can you offer an upgrade in shipping? Not all will respond positively, but some will. Usually this means changing words away from "you" and toward "what."

5—Not all solutions cost money or cost equal money. Remember my story about the customer where an issue could have cost me $4000 and instead cost me $2000? Why did it cost me less?

This is the same reason that stores offer store credit, not cash. Remember in your solution that "free shipping" might not cost the company what it would cost the customer. Some solutions only cost you your time. A discount on their next order costs only if they order again.

Part II. Everybody is different

Many of us are convinced we aren't good at handling difficult situations. We see other people 'get by' with strategies we can't use. The problem is not that we can't use those strategies, and more that we need to find what works for us. People are different; different strategies fit different people.

> *"I like to be by myself. Misery loves company."*
> *—Antonio "Tony Ducks" Corallo*

In fact situations are different too. So sometimes people and situations require different approaches. It's very important that you adopt a response that is comfortable to you and reduces your stress. In order for that to work, you should consider what your personality is like.

Consider the following metaphor. In this metaphor personalities are broken into a variety of types: **Athletes, Actors, Philosophers, Lovers, or Hermits.** If you can identify a personality that you feel 'is' you, then you can try strategies that may work for you.

"Never open your mouth, unless you're in the dentist chair" —Sammy "The Bull" Gravano

Of course most people feel that they somewhat fit two or more types. If that is true for you, it gives you several potential strategies to try. [2]

Athletes—*I know what I want and usually see the best way forward to solve problems. Usually people recognize me as the expert and listen.*

Just the facts

STRATEGY: *Just the Facts*. To make this strategy work, you need to have number based facts. You will look up the facts and reference written documents like bills and receipts.

The more you focus on the numbers the less stressed and emotional you will feel. If the customer still persists in being emotional/difficult, keep drawing their attention to the numbers. Once you both are

---

[2] This approach is based on the Thomas–Kilman Conflict Model

'working' on the numbers, the stress will decrease for both of you.

Actors—*I believe it's best to try to meet the needs of everybody involved. I listen carefully before I even state my position. Team solutions work best.*

L.E.A.R.N.

STRATEGY: *L.E.A.R.N.—Listen, Empathize, Apologize, React, and Now.* In this strategy you follow a path summarized in the acronym L.E.A.RN.

Focus yourself on listening first. Ask questions to make sure you understand the problem. Make sure you focus the other party on telling a complete, fact based story of what is wrong.

At the point where you feel you understand, introduce some empathy and a short reasonable apology,

> *"Mrs. Smith, I'm so sorry that we've encountered this problem."*

Craft your apology to be sincere, but not one that admits blame. Notice that it's a shared problem, not

Chapter 6: Tough Situations

theirs alone. You want to be on their side or impartial at best.

Now you want to aggressively leap into action. It's important that you take quick action. Lead with what you can do and why. Remain proactive. I suggest small steps that can be taken quickly.

You are building trust, so it's important that your first steps are timely and possible to accomplish correctly. Typical actions that can be accomplished quickly would be to say that you will call back within five minutes with an answer. Just be sure to actually call back!

Past, present, future

STRATEGY: *Past, Present, Future.* Here you would restate the problem. Keep your description very accurate and impartial, but state it as a 'past' problem.

> *"I understand Mr. Jones that you received the wrong product last Tuesday." Now talk about what now you can do to improve the future. "We can rush a replacement right out to you. You should receive it by Wednesday."*

Philosophers—*I believe that in conflicts everybody ought to give a little. That way we all win.*

50-50% solution

STRATEGY: *50-50% Solution.* Offer two lesser solutions to force a choice.

> *"We can do one of two things: give you a credit or ship you a replacement."*

> *"You can work reduced hours as long as you cover Monday. Or you can take the week off and be back to your regular schedule next week."*

Lovers—*I believe in looking at the other's guy's position. Sometimes I give away too much, but figure it's better to give it away rather than having angry people.*

Make an offer

STRATEGY: *Make an Offer.* For this solution, it is important to use a phrase like:

> *"How does that sound?"*

…or similar phrases. And it's important to learn to ask the question and then be quiet. By doing this you are putting the ball in their court.

Chapter 6: Tough Situations

"I can't reduce your hours, but you could work 10 hours 4 days a week, if that would help. How does that sound?" [pause]

Hermits—*I hate hurting anyone's feelings. If put in that position I usually get someone else to do it. Most problems that I've seen could have been avoided or seem trivial and not worth fighting about.*

Make it go away

STRATEGY: *Make it Go Away.* This strategy is far more powerful than people think. It involves allowing the other party to devise a solution. Keep in mind that you must feel free to say, "No," if the solution is not acceptable to you. You simply recognize the problem and say,

"Keeping in mind the limitations of my position, what would you think is a reasonable solution?"

Many times I've been surprised at how reasonable the ideas are. However, some people will hold out for the impossible, so you must be willing to say,

"That isn't possible, I wonder if we could—"

Part III—Understanding Negotiation

There are two types of negotiating: win-win and win-lose. Win-win negotiating is for cases when you value the relationship like marriage, customers, and employee-boss.

These are cases where you both need to come out undamaged and not seeking revenge or rematch. Clearly this type of negotiating needs trust.

Win-lose is for cases where you don't ever care to deal with the person again. For example, a used car purchase doesn't involve a long-term relationship. Some people argue that there are no places you should employ win-lose negotiating.

"Everybody has a price." —Jimmy Hoffa

There is another difference. Usually win-win negotiators have several items on the table. We talked about this in the chapter on salary negotiations.

Win-win negotiators put multiple items on the table and win-lose negotiators have only one. Usually money is the choice in win-lose. That's part of the reason that people fail in negotiating salary—they make it win-lose, and the boss has more perceived power.

But you can change that balance. The most powerful technique is to put something else on the

Chapter 6: Tough Situations

table. So for instance in a salary negotiation, add a discussion about vacation or training.

Tip 1—It's all about trust

You must do what you say and promptly. If you promise a follow-up the most damaging thing you can do is not follow-up.

Tip 2—Empathizing is not the same as admitting liability

Getting on their side doesn't mean admitting error or liability. Neither does apologizing. Apologize for their trouble. Offer to do what you can to make this right.

Tip 3—Thank them, yep, really!

A strangely powerful step is to thank them for bringing this to your attention. Frequently, this surprising action on your part will stop them in their tracks and change the tone of any further discussion.

Tip 4—You shouldn't expect to solve every problem

And when you can't solve a problem, generally you should escalate it to those who can, such as a manager.

There are three types of problems

1—Legitimate. Solve as above; be generous if you can.

EXAMPLE: I ordered a service, which wasn't delivered.

2—Legitimate, but beyond your control—for these, you solve the parts you can. Make sure that the customer is aware why you can't fix the parts out of your control. It is best if they come to the fair conclusion themselves.

EXAMPLE: Side effects from a medical treatment that require a visit to a specialist.

EXAMPLE: A tire store that can diagnose but not fix brake problems.

EXAMPLE: Product shipped that didn't arrive on schedule because of weather issue.

3—Illegitimate. Usually, this is a problem with the customer understanding what business you are in, or what role you play in the company. Use tact. Make sure the customer knows that you can see why they might be confused.

Chapter 6: Tough Situations

Offer either a source of better information for them and offer to promote the issue to others to resolve with better descriptions, signage etc.…

EXAMPLE: A doctor's office that doesn't accept Medicare.

Butch Cassidy: "Alright. I'll jump first."

Sundance Kid: "No."

Butch Cassidy: "Then you jump first."

Sundance Kid: "No, I said."

Butch Cassidy: "What's the matter with you?"

Sundance Kid: "I can't swim."

Butch Cassidy: "Are you crazy? The fall will probably kill you."

Sundance Kid: "Oh, shit..."

—"Butch Cassidy & the Sundance Kid"

Chapter 7: The Art of Being Accidentally Lucky

Make My Day

"The dream don't come no closer by itself. We gotta run after it now."
—Carlito, in "Carlito's Way"

You can pour blood, sweat and tears into reaching your dreams. Or you can just do it the easy way. Why are some people just plain lucky? And how can you steal a bit of their fairy dust and sprinkle it on yourself?

More and more people are feeling that they are looking at a smaller and smaller slice of the pie. They face tough financial times, a shrinking set of wages offered, and lots of compromises.

It's driving a sense of being worn out, obsolete and frankly—choice-less. It's even worse because we just emerged from a strong go-go period of endless opportunity where it seemed like everyone's wage rose and there were new opportunities. Worse still, a younger generation is seeing less opportunity than their parents or siblings saw.

A few years ago we were talking about the end of recessions and a new paradigm for the economy. Even professional economists questioned the business cycle and started saying that with the help of a few Federal Reserve tools we could have continual growth and low inflation.

Then, poof! That world became a discouraging world where houses don't always sell for more; it's a world where jobs are no longer guaranteed—where our savings seem vulnerable to just about everything.

And yet what has really changed? The sun rises and sets. The air is still there to breathe. Not many of us are starving. In fact a few people are doing quite well.

What do these people do differently? What is the difference between the people surviving and those who are thriving? Some very simple things: luck; willingness to change; a vision of what needs to change.

Let's talk about luck. Do you know a really lucky person? Someone who gets the best luck all the time? I know a few. I've studied them, because I'd like to help others become lucky.

My nephew Jim is studying for the Catholic priesthood. Of course, this means a life of simplicity, so money is not something he has much of. As a seminarian he's not permitted a job outside the seminary, so he and others studying survive on a small stipend of $2000 a year.

Recently when returning from an assignment working with the poor in the Honduras he and his fellows took a detour to the Caribbean. They paid for a

Chapter 7: The Art of Being Accidentally Lucky

few days stay from their meager funds and got a break as seminarians. And that's when the 'luck' seems to come in. They were then offered a few extra nights for free. Their hosts even drove them around the island and to the airport.

Why Jim? Well obviously he's nice to talk to. People come to trust him. He's smart, a great listener. And he's willing to consider things from a different way. Jim 'seems' lucky, but I think I know the source of his luck. If you knew him, you'd see it too.

Jim approaches life with an open heart and open mind. He sees advantages where others see difficulty. He offers his time without expecting reward. Oddly enough the reward follows anyway.

About the same time as Jim got his break, my son Tom also got a lucky break. He was working on a summer internship in Houston. While he was there he played on a company soccer team in a charity benefit.

The problem was that my son's team was heading to a tournament—after he had to be back at school at Purdue. One of his teammates volunteered to use her frequent flier miles to fly Tom back to Houston just for the tournament. Another offered to put him up and feed him for the weekend. A third offered to pick him up at the airport and get him back. They joked with him that he had to get three goals to pay them back. His team lost 5-3…but Tom had his three goals.

Why Tom? He had something to offer. He was likeable and reliable. He would be open to ideas.

One thing I've noticed about chronically 'lucky' people—they seem happy. Conversely I've noticed that chronically unlucky people seem unhappy.

You could argue that luck brings happiness, but you would then have one problem. People who are lucky just once, don't seem to be happy…and then forever lucky. People who are chronically happy seem to be chronically lucky.

Tip 1—Start off happy

So make your luck by seeing what there is to be happy for. Make yourself predisposed to being lucky, and then use that viewpoint to see opportunities.

Tip 2—Be good at something

Jim listens and obviously is helpful to talk to. It's a talent and a blessing. Tom is good at delivering what he promises. So you should have something to offer. Then offer it. Oddly—selling it is usually not as good so simply offering it.

I use this in business. I'm good at seeing artistic special effects solutions. I own and work for a special effects company.

Chapter 7: The Art of Being Accidentally Lucky

When I talk to customers, I don't worry at all about selling. I simply talk through creative solutions with customers. I don't care if my product is what they use. I tell them where to look, what to use, and give away hundreds of ideas for free.

I frequently give away artwork.[1] And, without fail, along the way I accidentally sell my product.

If you've ever had a job that requires selling, you probably learned to hate it. The quotas, the pressure of making sure that people are taken care of and happy are tough challenges. Wouldn't you rather 'accidentally' sell while solving someone's problem?

Many of you are thinking: Yes, but Tom and Jim are young and have their lives ahead of them. It's easy to be lucky you have everything ahead of you. Maybe, just maybe, that's backwards: what if they are lucky because they believe they have it all ahead of them?

I know a lady, Martha. She is amazing. She volunteers at the nursing home across the street from her condo. She pushes around the 'old folks' in their wheel chairs.

The 'old folks' are people in their seventies—which is a little odd, because Martha is 95. She was a newlywed when many of the 'old folks' were infants and toddlers. She helps out because she believes in

---

[1] A one time use of artwork; artists retain rights to future use.

service and helping those less fortunate. It's interesting to talk to Martha because she doesn't notice the ironies here. After a while of talking to her you might think that somebody forgot to tell her that she is a senior citizen—much less a nonagenarian.

I have a friend, Kit. She's also in her 90s and she dances twice a week. I love studying her. When someone needs a ride in our club, Kit drives the group. She fell broke her arm and recovered in weeks. She's absolutely amazing. She never stops.

Now one real paradox about Kit is that at 90 most people would say she has it all behind her—and yet she doesn't think that way. That can't be a coincidence. What if her drive to be doing something is part of what keeps her going?

Tip 3—Believe in something that's bigger than you
Tip 4—Believe in yourself

But then what if life throws you terrible curves? Martha and Kit are both widows. Martha had a husband sick for 20 years. Through no fault of his own, he lost his insurance. At the time he'd already experienced a massive heart attack.

She lay awake in bed for several weeks after he lost the insurance. She spend those long nights worrying. Then one night after some prayer she decided that the

Chapter 7: The Art of Being Accidentally Lucky

worst case would be that she'd go back to teaching. Typical of Martha, she thought, "Well I always liked teaching…I can live with that."

A young friend of mine has Lupus. She found out recently that it wasn't in remission as she had thought, and she had lost 50% of her kidney function. She was down for weeks—mostly because this might make pregnancy difficult and Ann wanted kids. She decided that this meant she'd be on a low salt diet for life.

The rest she decided would be something she'd find out later—there are specialists and women with Lupus sometimes manage to have kids. At least she knew what the battle was and could maybe salvage a future.

My friend Katie was a first time grandmother, mother of a teenager, just breaking into an art career, had a mother dying of a different reoccurrence of cancer—when she herself was diagnosed with breast cancer. She felt terribly guilty that she was thinking about herself and her cancer, rather than her mother, daughter or granddaughter.

She sought help, and found that the Prozac she was prescribed gained her a bit of perspective. She said it helped her see that if she knew where the bullet was coming from she could fight it (her words, not mine). She worked through the next few years and was cancer free five years later.

Tip 5—It's all about how you see things

If life throws the entire of bushels of lemons at you, decide on the worst case and build on that to improve your situation. Don't let this keep you down. Most successful 'lucky' people have had very 'unlucky' moments, but in those moments discovered unusual new perspectives.

Speaking of perspective, perspective can provide you with a way of seeing what needs to change. It can provide a game plan for the future.

The tough part is figuring out how to execute a Thriver's game plan. Say you are out of work, feeling anxious about that and feeling a bit unsuccessful. A Thriver would mourn that loss of job, but a few weeks later would decide they needed to change something.

They'd decide what was working for them and what was against them: the pros and cons of their life. So if they had a spouse and kids that loved them that would be a plus. God's love—then that's a plus too.

They decided that if they had their health, a roof over their head, a bit of savings, or even skills or determination they were doing well. What's temporary job loss compared to that?

OK, if the job is what do they need to change, then what would they be willing to do to get a job? Maybe

Chapter 7: The Art of Being Accidentally Lucky

move, work different hours, take a pay cut—are those the end of the world? No.

So with a vision of what needs to change and a willingness to change, this perspective will carry a Thriver forward.

Tip 6—Tell others about your hopes and dreams

Articulating your dreams increases their meaning to you, forces you to consider next steps and details. Articulation of those dreams to others also positions you to benefit from connections those other people may have. Dreams and hopes that are articulated have a higher likelihood of being achieved. Ironically, many people don't dare express their visions of the future, for fear that failure to achieve a goal would be seen as failure. If you define it as a failure it could be seen that way. So don't define it as a failure. A Thriver sees a path to the future where others would be looking at the path they've traveled.

Tip 7—Be generous with your skills and time

A Thriver will help others with whatever skill they have. A Thriver will be the guy volunteering at church or a food bank. A Thriver will be the one who is out and about doing things—and by doing so will be in the right position for the odd bone that life throws. It's interesting that people will acknowledge that luck is situational and temporal—you must be in the right place at the right time.

It's odd that people don't see that offering your skills more likely puts you in the right place to benefit.. Jim was there when the villa was offered. Tom was there when the tickets offered. Kit's dancing when other opportunities for travel present.

But just as a parting story…a little childhood insight into a natural Thriver. This is a story about the same nephew that is a seminarian. Jim when he was a child, was always coming home from Kindergarten with fresh cookies. His Dad asked one day how he managed to always have such tasty treats.

Five year-old Jim replied: "I know the cookie lady." Sometimes in life it helps to know the cookie lady. Most 'luck' comes from someone. Make a point of keeping your eyes open for different opportunities and know that buying cookies is not the only way to get cookies.

Chapter 7: The Art of Being Accidentally Lucky

"The world is changing and there are new opportunities for those who are ready to join forces with those who are stronger and more experienced."
—Charlie "Lucky" Luciano

Epilogue

How not to become a 90 year-old bank robber, or miscreant of any kind

Recently I watched a story of the 92-year-old bank robber, J. L Hunter "Red" Rountree. Red is an interesting character. He started as a successful businessman. As several personal tragedies befell him over several decades, he transformed from a regular upstanding citizen to an octogenarian thrill-seeker. He ended a crime spree in his nineties as a true rarity: a nonagenarian bank robber.

He first lost his business in bankruptcy for which he blamed the bank. Then, he lost his son in a car accident and finally he lost his wife of 50 years to cancer. This caused him to make a strong break from his here-to-fore respectable life. He started hanging out in strip joints and associating with less savory characters.

After taking up with a drug-addicted girlfriend, he first tried drugs, then fearing addiction became a thrill seeker who attempted greater and greater thrills in order to match the drug high.

His particular thrill was bank robbery. According to him, "It's fun!"

I can safely assume that my readers, like myself, are upstanding law abiding sorts very unlike Red. But there are lessons to be learned from Red's fall. In no particular order: people need a little risk taking (of course not at the additive levels of Red); life isn't over until it's over: new careers can start at any time; don't blame the system for your failure; life isn't fair; you can be what you choose to make of yourself.

So be careful what you make of yourself. Red was not a gangster like the others quoted in this book, but he does have one thing in common with the gangsters: Neither you nor I would want to be him.

"Judges, lawyers and politicians have a license to steal. We don't need one."
—*Carlo Gambino*

The Enlightened Entrepreneur

*Fortune Cookie Wisdom About
Starting Your Own Business*

Why fortune cookies?

I've always loved fortune cookies. They are slightly sweet, crunchy and have an interesting surprise. To a creative person the messages inside take twists and turns inside the mind until they find a nice sensible place to live. And if they are really good, they burrow inside your consciousness and—yes, I dare say that the good ones can influence your future behavior. And what does success depend on? Your success depends most on your future behavior.

Life does not get better by chance; it gets better by change. And did I mention that these cookies and messages are sweet? That helps too!

When you start a business, you will invariably encounter dozens of people with dire warnings for you. Many will predict impossible obstacles ahead. Some will cluck their tongues, look sincerely worried and mournfully state that they'd never do something this risky.

Always fond of small social experiments, I did a little informal count once when I was starting a new venture. I counted about nine 'naysayers' to every one 'yay-sayer.' This book doesn't join the ranks of negative advice givers. This book takes a positive approach to starting businesses and realizing entrepreneurial dreams. This book tells you the little positive secrets to staying on track to realize your dream of starting and growing a successful business.

You can succeed, and this book give you real advice to help you. Don't mistake the lighthearted approach for lack of meaningful business advice. We offer real advice that has saved businesses and fortunes—and happiness.

> *"Do not follow where the path may lead. Go where there is no path...and leave a trail." — Ralph Waldo Emerson*

BOOK EXCERPT—The Enlightened Entrepreneur

Chapter 1: Dreams

Rivers need springs

In the beginning, there is a dream. All businesses start here. I've heard dozens of dreams. When people hear that I've started two businesses, their eyes take on a different cast. (People see you differently if you've started a business.) Some eyes narrow and the faces that own those eyes ask questions about your business. A few are trying to see if that business is an eBay business (not that there is anything wrong with an eBay business!) so they can discount that experience. Once we get past that size question, many folks are curious, but a few want something more. They want advice. They want to vet their dreams.

So, 'yes,' I've heard dozens of dreams. Frequently, I'll share a coffee or lunch and just listen. If my companion wants advice, I'll extend advice. Sometimes I find that they only want to have someone to share their dream with—even for a few minutes. It seems as if dreaming is something that not everyone does. But I understand: If you dare to openly dream about something as audacious as starting a business, reactions from the workers of the world take on the character of the actions of crabs in a bucket—should one crab develop an ambition to leave the bucket, the others drag him back down!

Many who dream, dream only to experience that dream-state of 'what-if?' They like the idea of having an idea. But others really want to consider a different life. They want to be entrepreneurs.

What a dream! To create a business from scratch. To take an idea that you own, to cradle it in your hands and to bring it to life. To sweat, and toil to grow this creation to maturity. Then to live the dream for decades and perhaps even to have your creation survive past your lifetime.

Of those great dreamers I find commonly two types. And I find myself searching and hoping for a third type. As the dreamer talks about his dream business, I find myself classifying him.

Type 1: Some dream the dream of a great idea

The first type of potential-entrepreneurs have an idea that they love. Let me restate that: they have an idea that they LOVE! For them this love is a true love. They will hold onto this idea through rain, sleet, tornados, frogs, and locust.

They very well may be right and the idea may be worthy of their devotion. The idea may be fantastic. And

BOOK EXCERPT—The Enlightened Entrepreneur

sometimes it isn't. Or it's almost-fantastic, just missing one piece of technology or just missing an audience that understands it's potential. They aren't alone. Many people would cite Thomas Edison as one of the greatest inventors of all time. Of course he invented the light bulb, and the phonograph. Great ideas, right? But have you heard of the electric pen? Edison noticed that the stylus of telegraph, which he invented, left a mark on the surface below it. He realized that if he made a pen that perforated a piece of paper that the paper could be used as a pattern to duplicate the document. Since this was long before Xerox and before the use of even mimeograph machines, Edison saw this as a real opportunity.

Have you heard of the electric pen? Nope, few know about it. It didn't take off as a product. And of course Edison couldn't understand that. However, the electric pen did spawn something else. 135 years after Edison created the electric pen, you can see something very similar to the electric pen used to apply tattoos. Can you imagine Edison with a tattoo? It'd be a light bulb, right? Now tattoos are now big business.

Learn from both Edison's successes and failures. You can succeed with ideas you love. You simply must keep your eyes open to strengths and weaknesses. It's a lot like raising great kids. You can't turn a blind eye to their actions, just because you love them. Even if you love an idea, you must see how other people see that idea. Learn to take the great ideas to the great market for those ideas.

To succeed, the customer for your idea must come to understand and love it as much as you do. The great idea may be a process improvement. Frequently I've seen people that want to apply an advanced manufacturing idea to a less advanced industry or market. Most often I hear about applying Six-Sigma ideas[1] to other markets and industries.

Most people would agree that this is a great idea. The key to making it work is to understand the market and the numbers. Can the cost of that process truly pay for itself?

Improvements should sell more products or cut your cost, or they aren't viable improvements.

Another dream I've heard is the great idea to bring a new flavor to a restaurant or a new product line to a store. Perhaps you want to bring an Indian restaurant to a small town.

There is nothing wrong with bringing a flavor of home to a new hometown or variety to an environment. This can be a wonderful idea. If you want the idea to work, do your homework and see if other people want an Indian restaurant.

---

[1] Six-Sigma is a statistical method to improve a manufacturing process.

BOOK EXCERPT—The Enlightened Entrepreneur

My niece opened a children's/baby store to a distant Canadian province, with great success. She brought her dream to life by filling a need. She also is very savvy about seeing needs and styles that people desire. She is now opening a second store.

Type one entrepreneurs do succeed. They succeed more often if they keep their ideas in perspective.

Type 2: Some dream the dream of a lifestyle

Many people that I talk to don't know what business to start. That may surprise you, but I see it all the time. These folks love their idea of the entrepreneur's lifestyle. Many simply want respect. A few expect vast benefits of ownership. Many want freedom to explore ideas. Many want to run a business their way. Some of these people have seen dishonesty, or unethical practices. Some have seen poor treatment of employees or customers. Many want to remedy such wrongs. Some simply want to run a business under terms favorable to them. So perhaps they don't want to work on Sunday. Or they need to work around their children's school schedules.

In some ways, type two entrepreneurs have an advantage over type ones. Type two folks can match the business to the demand. If they see a need, they can meet it. Their analysis can be dispassionate.

Type twos encounter two very real problems. First, they frequently don't have any real idea at all what business to start. Second, most of them will restrict the types of businesses they will start—usually they want the more glamorous or prestigious option. Not many are interested in being the garbage-collection service.

Usually these entrepreneurs are best asking themselves what they like; what they excel at and what is truly missing in their world. It's also good to be aware of what exactly they like about an entrepreneur's lifestyle. Bill was a friend of mine. For many years he knew I had started businesses. And for many years he dreamed of an entrepreneurial life. As a manufacturing engineer, he had a high stress job. He dealt with unmanageable deadlines, unions, long hours, around the clock responsibilities and bosses (irrational, psychopaths by his description) who multiplied like rabbits. After 30 years in the field, he'd had it. A local garage came up for sale and Bill dreamed of buying it, turning around the business and specializing on performance modifications to vehicles.

Can Bill succeed? 'Yes' he can and will. He's demonstrated a strong capability to analyze the business details when he produced a complete inventory and an analysis of the capacity and usage of the current space. But success will come easier if he tempers his strong need to leave his current work.

He needs to take the time to make sure that he buys the garage at a price that is reasonable. He will

BOOK EXCERPT—The Enlightened Entrepreneur

further increase his odds of success if he has established that there is a market for his business.

My first advice to Bill was to plan his retirement and his daughter's college education. Once he knows how he's going to retire and provide for her, then he can be free to develop a realistic business plan.

He wisely structured a deal to purchase the garage that delayed some of the purchase and made the price conditional on his first five years of success. And he's chosen a business that his skills and interest match.

More commonly people don't have an idea of what business they might thrive in. And many of them won't consider some occupations. Years ago I read an article in the Wall Street Journal about a reunion of Harvard Business School grads.

They compared salaries. The best paid was a gentlemen who owned a garbage-collection business. I'm not surprised. I bet he has a big yacht and a big house in the Bahamas and time off work—and I'll bet he laughs on his way to the bank. Many businesses that seem less desirable have stronger profit potential.

I know plenty of artists: Most don't make money. I know a few suppliers of materials to artists: they do make money.

I don't think that's a coincidence. If somebody likes playing the guitar, they dream of playing music as a professional musician.

The problem is that not many people can succeed in the field and even less can make money or have a great lifestyle. However, there are lots of successful businesses built around the music industry.

Tip 1—Look at your interests; then look to businesses that supply people pursuing that interest

Instead of being the guitarist, think about what guitarists need to succeed and provide that.

Type 3: Some are naturals

There is a third type of entrepreneur that I look for. I call that type 'naturals.' Oddly enough, naturals aren't born, they seem to be made.

Frequently, they've started or tried to start a business before. Almost as frequently they have failed.

Occasionally, I find one that simply has a nature that incorporates the traits needed to be a natural. With a small handful, I've been able to coach them to adopt the traits needed.

Among those traits I include are: passion, dispassionate analysis, a willingness to accept ideas you don't like, a willingness to reject ideas you like, and an ability to look beyond yourself for help.

BOOK EXCERPT—The Enlightened Entrepreneur

Tip 2—Temper your passion with reason

A natural may love their idea, but still can modify it or discard it if needed. They are on the hunt for improvements and will find improvements in all sorts of places. Recently an organic baby food maker was in the news. She had started her business in one of the toughest business environments ever—retail food.

She was struggling until she hit upon a packaging that made her product cost-effective and convenient. Most people would have given up when they couldn't make jars of baby food profitable. She had an open mind and was looking for solutions. She settled on an economical pouch. That small change made her business successful.

I've had to constantly modify my product to stay in business. I've borrowed ideas from different industries and constantly look at how other products are constructed. I'm always testing new materials. I've made several changes in response to new ideas.

None of these ideas look revolutionary, but they've shaved time and cost off of manufacturing my product. We make a special effect product called scrim. For years it's been made the same way with the same materials.

My company changed what it was made of and how it was constructed and in the process made it easier and faster to make a custom product. Like the baby food manufacturer, my small business has innovated in manufacturing, packaging, labeling, marketing as well as production of products.

Tip 3—Pursue ideas that can provide you a living

If a business cannot support you, it's a hobby. Interests in hobbies tend to fade, so how can you expect to continue a business for any length of time if your interest fades?

And you can't expect to sell something to someone else if your interest has faded. To have a real successful business, your customers must pay enough for the product/improvement to support you.

Naturals test markets, run numbers, and check opinions. If at all possible these entrepreneurs conduct a dry run with customers.

Before my company was founded, my hardworking partner took the product door to door to test it with dozens of high-end professionals. After several months she delivered dozens of testimonials and photographs of the product in use.

When this trial period was over, we had a great idea of the price to charge for the product and dozens of creative uses for it. We also had information about popular sizes and colors, disadvantages and advantages.

BOOK EXCERPT—The Enlightened Entrepreneur

Most importantly we now had some information about whether we could sell at a profit and enough of a profit to support us.

Tip 4—Keep looking for even better ways

Many businesspeople would say that the cardinal rule of business is: improve or die. Having one idea is never enough. You must be able to constantly experiment and improve. Listen for how your customers use your product. Listen for how customers modify your product. Listen to complaints against your product. If someone complains that the product doesn't deliver fast enough, consider and reconsider your options for delivery.

Tip 5—Everything is a partnership

My partner was not my partner in name or even legally. She was my graphic designer and worked to launch my product and acted as my representative.

Naturals come to understand that suppliers and distributors are your partners. What you can't deliver, they may be able to.

The relationship with my designer was a key relationship to my business. I greatly valued it. But even smaller relationships can be key. For years I dodged my FedEx representative when she called.

Finally, I realized that if I dared to ask, that she just might help me. The more our business has grown, the more FedEx has become a strategic partner allowing us to deliver custom products in days and have the shortest delivery time in our industry.

Tip 6—Keep dreaming

Savor the feeling of having a dream. Use that feeling to drive you. And when the dream begins to flag, take some time to dream some more. The energy level of an entrepreneur is their secret weapon.

Follow your bliss and the Universe will open doors where there were once only walls.

Copyright 2014 Susan Riehle

About the Author

Susan Riehle is the founder of two companies. She works for one of those companies, Studio Productions, Inc. a special effects company. She speaks on topics of employment, leadership and entrepreneurship.

Susan has advised dozens of individuals, companies and non-profit organizations in ways to be more effective and happy.

Susan Riehle draws on her conversations with dozens of people and her own wide set of experiences. She has:

✧ Founded two companies, including Studio Productions, Inc. which she started 23 years ago. Under her direction, Studio Productions has become a major producer of theatrical scrims, projection surfaces; and is the premier producer of printed scrims.

✧ Holds a BSEE (Electrical Engineering) and a MBA, and has managed large software teams distributed over three continents.

- ✧ Has an impressive artistic resume as a set designer with years of experience designing sets for various theatrical venues.

- ✧ Has a 30 year resume as a teacher in Software Programming and other engineering topics including Robotics.

- ✧ Is known as a vocal and active board member and an adviser for local not-for-profit organizations and for a college in Indiana.

- ✧ Volunteers her time advising on interviewing and mock interviewing, as well as advising professionals on career strategy.

Susan draws upon all her experiences to convey the lessons of a full life and a productive, satisfying life–encouraging others to run, not walk and inhale deeply the oxygen of living.

bullet points

Quick Reference Guide

Wise Guy Tips

Job Search

Be a specialist—just the right specialist. Don't apply for just any job. Tailor your resume to the kind of job that excites you and that you can do well.

Look for the nexus. The best jobs are found at the intersection between two types of expertise. Typically this means a skill set and an industry. So a software engineer with understanding of a niche such as the automotive industry has an edge over even the best software engineer.

Learn how to read a job posting. Learn to distinguish between the parts of the posting written by the legal and HR departments and those written by the job poster. The supervisor will have written key details that help you prepare for the interview.

Interviewing

Know the job. Know the company. Know the interviewer. If you know only the interviewer's name you haven't researched enough—and don't deserve the job.

There is really only one questioned asked in any interview. The question is, "Why should I hire you for this job?" Prepare for that question asked in any possible way realizing that the question may be asked in several coded forms (Where do you see yourself in five years? Tell me about a prior conflict at work?)

Nervous? Make an interview into a conversation to calm your nerves—and to make the interviewer comfortable, too. You can do this by asking questions. Try, "What do you like about working here?" If possible, work up to the question, "What are you looking for in an employee?"

Trust you! Build trust during the interview by showing that you are someone who has been trusted. You do this by playing up any increases in responsibility that you have earned in past positions. This can be handling money, important customers or assignments or being asked to train others.

Don't throw away experience. What you learn from prior jobs in different careers is important—it's a simple matter of showing what you learned from these jobs that applies to job you want. If you discount this experience, everyone will.

Negotiating

Know your job classification. And know the classification of the job you want. (Check these on Salary.com) Your job in the negotiation is to move closer to the second in terms of responsibility and qualifications. Your boss can help you do that.

Always put more than one thing on the table. Salary is just one of the things to discuss. Also discuss job flexibility, hours, and future opportunities and responsibilities.

Always position yourself as simply seeking fair and equitable terms. Then be flexible in how you reach this goal.

think
upside
down™

www.ingramcontent.com/pod-product-compliance
Lightning Source LLC
LaVergne TN
LVHW051121080426
835510LV00018B/2171